# Walt Whitman

# The Selected Poems
## *of*
# WALT WHITMAN

*Published for The Classics Club by*

WALTER J. BLACK · NEW YORK

This book is a choice of
The Classics Club
Selection Committee

# Contents

INTRODUCTION                                              xiii

INSCRIPTIONS
    ONE'S-SELF I SING                             1
    IN CABIN'D SHIPS AT SEA                       1
    TO FOREIGN LANDS                              3
    WHEN I READ THE BOOK                          3
    ME IMPERTURBE                                 4
    I HEAR AMERICA SINGING                        4
    SHUT NOT YOUR DOORS                           5

STARTING FROM PAUMANOK                                     6

SONG OF MYSELF                                            25

CHILDREN OF ADAM
    TO THE GARDEN THE WORLD                     111
    ONE HOUR TO MADNESS AND JOY                 111
    OUT OF THE ROLLING OCEAN THE CROWD          113
    AGES AND AGES RETURNING AT INTERVALS        114
    WE TWO, HOW LONG WE WERE FOOL'D             114
    O HYMEN! O HYMENEE!                         115
    ONCE I PASS'D THROUGH A POPULOUS CITY       115
    I HEARD YOU SOLEMN-SWEET PIPES OF THE
        ORGAN                                116
    FACING WEST FROM CALIFORNIA'S SHORES        117
    AS ADAM EARLY IN THE MORNING                117

# CALAMUS

IN PATHS UNTRODDEN 118
SCENTED HERBAGE OF MY BREAST 119
WHOEVER YOU ARE HOLDING ME NOW IN HAND 121
FOR YOU O DEMOCRACY 124
THESE I SINGING IN SPRING 124
NOT HEAVING FROM MY RIBB'D BREAST ONLY 126
OF THE TERRIBLE DOUBT OF APPEARANCES 127
THE BASE OF ALL METAPHYSICS 128
RECORDERS AGES HENCE 129
ARE YOU THE NEW PERSON DRAWN TOWARD
    ME? 130
ROOTS AND LEAVES THEMSELVES ALONE 131
NOT HEAT FLAMES UP AND CONSUMES 131
TRICKLE DROPS 132
CITY OF ORGIES 133
TO A STRANGER 133
THIS MOMENT YEARNING AND THOUGHTFUL 134
I HEAR IT WAS CHARGED AGAINST ME 135
THE PRAIRIE-GRASS DIVIDING 135
WHEN I PERUSE THE CONQUER'D FAME 136
A PROMISE TO CALIFORNIA 136
HERE THE FRAILEST LEAVES OF ME 137
NO LABOR-SAVING MACHINE 137
A LEAF FOR HAND IN HAND 138
EARTH, MY LIKENESS 138
I DREAM'D IN A DREAM 138
TO THE EAST AND TO THE WEST 139
SOMETIMES WITH ONE I LOVE 139
FAST-ANCHOR'D ETERNAL O LOVE! 140
AMONG THE MULTITUDE 140
FULL OF LIFE NOW 140

SONG OF THE OPEN ROAD 142

CROSSING BROOKLYN FERRY 158

SONG OF THE ANSWERER                                    168

SONG OF THE BROAD-AXE                                   175

PIONEERS! O PIONEERS!                                   191

YEAR OF METEORS (1859–60)                               197

A BROADWAY PAGEANT                                      199

SEA-DRIFT
    OUT OF THE CRADLE ENDLESSLY ROCKING          205
    AS I EBB'D WITH THE OCEAN OF LIFE            214
    TEARS                                        218
    ON THE BEACH AT NIGHT                        218
    THE WORLD BELOW THE BRINE                    220
    ON THE BEACH AT NIGHT ALONE                  221
    SONG FOR ALL SEAS, ALL SHIPS                 222
    PATROLING BARNEGAT                           224
    AFTER THE SEA-SHIP                           224
    WHEN I HEARD THE LEARN'D ASTRONOMER          225

DRUM-TAPS
    FIRST O SONGS FOR A PRELUDE                  226
    EIGHTEEN SIXTY-ONE                           229
    BEAT! BEAT! DRUMS!                           231
    FROM PAUMANOK STARTING I FLY LIKE A BIRD     232
    SONG OF THE BANNER AT DAYBREAK               233
    RISE O DAYS FROM YOUR FATHOMLESS DEEPS       242
    VIRGINIA—THE WEST                            245
    CITY OF SHIPS                                246
    THE CENTENARIAN'S STORY                      247
    CAVALRY CROSSING A FORD                      253
    BIVOUAC ON A MOUNTAIN SIDE                   254
    AN ARMY CORPS ON THE MARCH                   255
    BY THE BIVOUAC'S FITFUL FLAME                255
    COME UP FROM THE FIELDS FATHER               256
    VIGIL STRANGE I KEPT ON THE FIELD ONE
        NIGHT                                    258

# DRUM-TAPS

## (*Continued*)

A MARCH IN THE RANKS HARD-PREST, AND
    THE ROAD UNKNOWN      260
A SIGHT IN CAMP IN THE DAYBREAK GRAY
    AND DIM      262
AS TOILSOME I WANDER'D VIRGINIA'S WOODS      263
NOT THE PILOT      264
YEAR THAT TREMBLED AND REEL'D BENEATH
    ME      264
THE WOUND-DRESSER      265
LONG, TOO LONG AMERICA      269
GIVE ME THE SPLENDID SILENT SUN      269
DIRGE FOR TWO VETERANS      272
OVER THE CARNAGE ROSE PROPHETIC A
    VOICE      274
I SAW OLD GENERAL AT BAY      275
THE ARTILLERYMAN'S VISION      276
ETHIOPIA SALUTING THE COLORS      278
NOT YOUTH PERTAINS TO ME      279
RACE OF VETERANS      279
WORLD TAKE GOOD NOTICE      279
O TAN-FACED PRAIRIE-BOY      280
LOOK DOWN FAIR MOON      280
RECONCILIATION      280
HOW SOLEMN AS ONE BY ONE      281
AS I LAY WITH MY HEAD IN YOUR LAP
    CAMERADO      282
DELICATE CLUSTER      282
TO A CERTAIN CIVILIAN      283
LO, VICTRESS ON THE PEAKS      284
SPIRIT WHOSE WORK IS DONE      284
ADIEU TO A SOLDIER      285
TURN O LIBERTAD      286
TO THE LEAVEN'D SOIL THEY TROD      287

MEMORIES OF PRESIDENT LINCOLN

     WHEN LILACS LAST IN THE DOORYARD BLOOM'D 289
     O CAPTAIN! MY CAPTAIN!     302
     HUSH'D BE THE CAMPS TO-DAY     303
     THIS DUST WAS ONCE THE MAN     304

THERE WAS A CHILD WENT FORTH     305

TO A FOIL'D EUROPEAN REVOLUTIONAIRE     308

PROUD MUSIC OF THE STORM     311

PASSAGE TO INDIA     320

PRAYER OF COLUMBUS     334

DAREST THOU NOW O SOUL     338

TO ONE SHORTLY TO DIE     339

THOU MOTHER WITH THY EQUAL BROOD     340

TO A LOCOMOTIVE IN WINTER     349

SO LONG!     351

WITH HUSKY-HAUGHTY LIPS, O SEA!     356

# Introduction

A FAVORITE subject for painters in the nineteenth century was an imaginary assemblage of the great American authors gathered in dignified conference for the edification of future ages. The pictures are less important as works of art than as evidence of which writers then seemed certain of lasting fame. The scene is usually a library, with velvet hangings, marble busts, and richly bound volumes—an appropriate expression of the derivative character of our early literature. Longfellow, of course, occupies a position of honor, with Bryant, Whittier, Emerson, Lowell, and Holmes not far away. Grouped about them are a host of lesser writers like N. P. Willis, Lydia Sigourney, and many others, now completely forgotten. They are all carefully dressed and comport themselves with the genteel conformity so manifest in their works. If he appears at all, Poe is to be found alone, placed in the background aloof from his more respectable contemporaries, whose grave disapproval of his intemperate habits tended to include his poetry as well.

One figure—a greater poet than any—is never included in these pictures: Walt Whitman. His entrance into such a circle of silk waistcoats, kid gloves, and top hats would have caused as much consternation as the appearance of *Leaves of Grass.* He stood over six feet tall, tipping the scales at two hundred pounds, a healthy, athletic-looking man, who would not have been abashed in any society. Though scrupulously clean, he looked like a day laborer in his heavy boots, baggy trousers, coarse shirt open at the neck, battered felt hat with broad brim, and coat slung loosely over one arm. In contrast to this scholarly gathering, he was conspicuously an out-of-doors man, with ruddy, tanned face and forehead, blue eyes that seemed to absorb whatever they rested on, and a full beard years before beards of any sort had come into fashion.

His poetry was as revolutionary as his appearance. The list of suitable subjects he augmented to include anything in the universe. For the conventional poetic diction with its archaisms and clichés he substituted the vigorous daily speech of the common American. Worst of all, it seemed to his contemporaries, he abandoned rhyme and the ordinary rhythms in favor of free verse. Moreover, he gloried in being different:

> *I too am not a bit tamed, I too am untranslatable,*
> *I sound my barbaric yawp over the roofs of the world.*

What can explain this remarkable person, whose poems are a turning-point in American literature?

Walt Whitman was born May 31, 1819, on a farm near Huntington, Long Island. His mother was of Dutch-American ancestry, his father, a Quaker, a carpenter by trade. Four years later the family moved to Brooklyn, where Walt attended public school until his twelfth year. He was then set to learning the printer's trade, which, combined with newspaper editing, formed his principal occupation for twenty years. His early verses, contributed to the papers for which he worked, show little promise of his remarkable powers.

During the presidential campaign of 1848 his antipathy to Negro slavery cost him the position he had held for two years as editor of the Brooklyn *Daily Eagle,* whose owners opposed the Free Soilers. With his brother Whitman journeyed to New Orleans to work for the *Daily Crescent.* Within a few months he was back in Brooklyn, writing for various newspapers and helping his father build houses. In his lunch box he carried a book to read during the noon hour. His mind was teeming with thoughts for poems of a new kind. On July 4, 1855, he issued a volume of them under the title *Leaves of Grass.*

One of the first copies Whitman sent to Ralph Waldo Emerson, whose *Essays* had greatly influenced him. "I was simmering, simmering," he said; "Emerson brought me to a boil." In many respects *Leaves of Grass* follows the pattern Emerson drew for the American poet of the future. His subject should be not the great, the remote, the romantic; he was to embrace the common, to explore and sit at the feet of the familiar, the low. "What would we really know the meaning of?" Emerson asked. "The meal in the firkin; the milk in the pan; the ballad in the street; the news of the boat; the glance of the eye; the form and the gait of the body." Whitman took the common, the familiar, the low for his subject. In his own way, too, he adopted the functional form Emerson advocated in his essay on the Poet: "It is not metres, but metre-making argument, that makes a poem—a thought so passionate and alive that like the spirit of a plant or an animal, it has an architecture of its own."

"I look in vain for the poet whom I describe," he added. ". . . We have yet had no genius in America with tyrannous eye which knew the value of our incomparable materials. . . . Banks and tariffs, the newspaper and caucus, methodism and unitarianism, are flat and dull to dull people, but rest on the same foundations of wonder as the town of Troy and the temple of Delphos, and are as swiftly passing away. Our log-rolling, our stumps and their politics, our fisheries, our Negroes and Indians, our boats, our repudiations, the wrath of rogues and the pusillanimity of honest men, the northern trade, the southern planting, the western clearing, Oregon and Texas are yet unsung. Yet America is a poem in our eyes; its ample geography dazzles the imagination, and it will not wait long for metres."

When *Leaves of Grass* came to his hands, Emerson was amazed to see this hope realized. Never had his beliefs been so boldly exemplified. Whitman accepted the fundamental idea of the Oversoul:

*Divine I am inside and out, and I make holy whatever I touch or*
*am touch'd from.*

In "Self-Reliance" Emerson had written: "Man is timid and apologetic; he is no longer upright; he dares not say 'I think,' 'I am,' but quotes some saint or sage. He is ashamed before the blade of grass or the blowing rose." But no one could accuse Walt Whitman of timidity. Believing that "self-existence is the attribute of the Supreme Cause," he wrote confidently of himself:

> *I celebrate myself, and sing myself,*
> *And what I assume you shall assume,*
> *For every atom belonging to me as good belongs to you.*
> *       . . . I permit to speak at every hazard,*
> *Nature without check with original energy.*

This is not egotism in the ordinary sense, for in himself Whitman sees all other men too, identifying himself with each in turn:

> *I am the hounded slave, I wince at the bite of the dogs. . . .*
> *I do not ask the wounded person how he feels, I myself become*
> *       the wounded person. . . .*
> *I am the mash'd fireman with breast-bone broken. . . .*
> *I am the man, I suffer'd, I was there.*

The divinity linking all men thus becomes the prototype of democracy. In an age of flowery titles Whitman chose to call his book *Leaves of Grass* to emphasize the universal aspect. He wanted his poems to be within reach of every one, spreading and growing like grass, the commonest yet most indispensable plant. He wanted "to define America, her athletic democracy."

*Is it you that thought the President greater than you?*
*Or the rich better off than you? or the educated wiser than*
*    you? . . .*
*The sum of all known reverence I add up in you whoever you are.*

Whitman extended this equality even to the sexes. To the world of 1855 it was startling to be told that

*It is as great to be a woman as to be a man.*

The conventional assumption that woman's place was in the home was challenged by his ideal picture of the great city,

*Where women walk in public processions in the streets the same*
*    as the men,*
*Where they enter the public assembly and take places the same*
*    as the men.*

More disturbing was Whitman's insistence that all parts of the body were equally noble.

*Welcome is every organ and attribute of me, and of any man*
*    hearty and clean,*
*Not an inch nor a particle of an inch is vile, and none shall be*
*    less familiar than the rest.*

This consistent frankness was enough in an age of prudery and euphemism to unleash charges of immorality from every quarter. Whitman stood many years ahead of his time. Modern writers owe much of their freedom to portray the whole of human life to his resolute refusal to yield. He was deeply sincere, and the world has since gathered about him. Yet we must sympathize with his contemporaries, who were genuinely shocked; we must concede that Whitman was somewhat deficient in the common human instinct of reticence. As one critic remarked of *Leaves of Grass*: "Here be all kinds of leaves but fig leaves."

The most perplexing side of Whitman is found in the Calamus poems, which celebrate the "manly love of comrades." To judge them fairly one must bear in mind that they were written in a period of romantic sentimentality; fraternal orders were springing up everywhere, and in the colleges secret societies swelled with the first floods of brotherly love. Liberty and Equality had had their day; now Whitman proposed to give Fraternity its due. In spite of the robust tone of these poems, the modern reader sees in them evidence of an arrested emotional development that left Whitman in some respects an adolescent. He is like a boy in his desire to shock, in his exhibitionism, his buoyant athleticism. There is something childlike in his imaginative identification of himself with others—the soldier, the ship captain, the fireman, the locomotive engineer, the hunter, and even the bear in quick succession. To this same level of development may be ascribed his failure to distinguish clearly between love for a woman and the love of comrades. Perhaps he recognized that poetry had its source in the remote depths of his mind and cultivated a profound ignorance of his own psychology for fear of destroying the spring. Other poets—the Shakespeare of the Sonnets, for example—have presented the same problem.

This phase of Whitman's poetry passed after the beginning of the Civil War, when his hunger for comradeship was sublimated in volunteer service among the sick and wounded. Primitive hygiene was causing more deaths than bullets. There was no well-organized system of relief; one society, aiming to prepare the sufferers for the next world rather than to make them comfortable in this, distributed 787,276 pages of religious tracts, but only 7,500 pages of writing paper and no tobacco. Having come to Washington when his brother was wounded, Whitman stayed on to do what he could in the hospitals. Every day he visited the wards, passing from cot to cot to talk with each man, jotting down memoranda in his notebook. The next day he would appear with fruit, candy, tobacco, stationery, stamps, etc. for those who needed them. He would sit by a wounded boy's bed, writing a letter home for him, and by his own intense vitality instilling courage to live. The army doctors and hundreds of their patients acknowledged Whitman as the force that turned the balance towards life at the critical moment. Emerson and other friends sent him money for supplies, which Whitman supplemented by writing for the newspapers.

Although the work was important in itself, the emotional tension it involved provided extraordinary material for poems. Democracy took on a deeper significance for Whitman through his personal association with men from every part of "these United States." Long years in the constant presence of death focused sharply in him the sorrow felt in a million American homes. When President Lincoln was assassinated he expressed the nation's grief in "When Lilacs Last in the Dooryard Bloom'd," which (though less popular than the melodramatic rhymed piece "O Captain! My Captain!" commemorating the same loss) is Whitman's finest poem. Like all the other works, these were added to *Leaves of Grass.*

After the war Whitman held a clerkship in the Attorney General's office until 1873, when he suffered a stroke of paralysis. He moved to Camden, New Jersey, living for eleven years with his brother. The remaining eight years of his life were spent in a house of his own at 328 Mickle Street, where many distinguished visitors called to pay their respects to "the Good Gray Poet." He continued to add poems to *Leaves of Grass,* of which the tenth edition appeared before his death, March 26, 1892.

Every new form of art has had to struggle against the opposition of critics who are too much preoccupied with the old. Whitman's poetry was ridiculed in much the same way as the music of his contemporary Richard Wagner. The free verse, the outspoken frankness, and the supposed ob-

scurity of his thought postponed for many years the gen-
eral recognition of his greatness. But these factors no longer
hinder readers, and in the opinion of most modern critics
Whitman stands as the greatest American poet of the nine-
teenth century. Compared to his, the work of Bryant,
Whittier, and Longfellow lacks vigor and substance. By a
curious paradox the common man for whom he wrote pre-
ferred the mild sweetness of "Snowbound" and "The Vil-
lage Blacksmith" to Whitman's turbulent music. But he
waited unperturbed:

*Whether I come into my own today or in ten thousand or ten
    million years,
I can cheerfully take it now, or with equal cheerfulness I can wait.*

GORDON S. HAIGHT

*Come, said my Soul,*
*Such verses for my Body let us write, (for we are one,)*
*That should I after death invisibly return,*
*Or, long, long hence, in other spheres,*
*There to some group of mates the chants resuming,*
*(Tallying Earth's soil, trees, winds, tumultuous waves,)*
*Ever with pleas'd smile I may keep on,*
*Ever and ever yet the verses owning—as, first, I here and now,*
*Signing for Soul and Body, set to them my name,*

*Walt Whitman*

# Inscriptions

## ONE'S-SELF I SING

One's-self I sing, a simple separate person,
Yet utter the word Democratic, the word En-Masse.

Of physiology from top to toe I sing,
Not physiognomy alone nor brain alone is worthy for the
    Muse, I say the Form complete is worthier far,
The Female equally with the Male I sing.

Of Life immense in passion, pulse, and power,
Cheerful, for freest action form'd under the laws divine,
The Modern Man I sing.

## IN CABIN'D SHIPS AT SEA

In cabin'd ships at sea,
The boundless blue on every side expanding,
With whistling winds and music of the waves, the large
    imperious waves,

I

Or some lone bark buoy'd on the dense marine,
Where joyous full of faith, spreading white sails,
She cleaves the ether mid the sparkle and the foam of day,
    or under many a star at night,
By sailors young and old haply will I, a reminiscence of the
    land, be read,
In full rapport at last.


*Here are our thoughts, voyagers' thoughts,*
*Here not the land, firm land, alone appears, may then by*
    *them be said,*
*The sky o'erarches here, we feel the undulating deck be-*
    *neath our feet,*
*We feel the long pulsation, ebb and flow of endless motion,*
*The tones of unseen mystery, the vague and vast suggestions*
    *of the briny world, the liquid-flowing syllables,*
*The perfume, the faint creaking of the cordage, the*
    *melancholy rhythm,*
*The boundless vista and the horizon far and dim are all here,*
*And this is ocean's poem.*


Then falter not O book, fulfil your destiny,
You not a reminiscence of the land alone,
You too as a lone bark cleaving the ether, purpos'd I know
    not whither, yet ever full of faith,
Consort to every ship that sails, sail you!
Bear forth to them folded my love, (dear mariners, for you
    I fold it here in every leaf;)
Speed on my book! spread your white sails my little bark
    athwart the imperious waves,

2

Chant on, sail on, bear o'er the boundless blue from me to
       every sea,
This song for mariners and all their ships.


## TO FOREIGN LANDS

I heard that you ask'd for something to prove this puzzle the
       New World,
And to define America, her athletic Democracy,
Therefore I send you my poems that you behold in them
       what you wanted.


## WHEN I READ THE BOOK

When I read the book, the biography famous,
And is this then (said I) what the author calls a man's life?
And so will some one when I am dead and gone write my
       life?
(As if any man really knew aught of my life,
Why even I myself I often think know little or nothing of
       my real life,
Only a few hints, a few diffused faint clews and indirections
I seek for my own use to trace out here.)

# ME IMPERTURBE

Me imperturbe, standing at ease in Nature,
Master of all or mistress of all, aplomb in the midst of
    irrational things,
Imbued as they, passive, receptive, silent as they,
Finding my occupation, poverty, notoriety, foibles, crimes,
    less important than I thought,
Me toward the Mexican sea, or in the Mannahatta or the
    Tennessee, or far north or inland,
A river man, or a man of the woods or of any farm-life of
    these States or of the coast, or the lakes or Kanada,
Me wherever my life is lived, O to be self-balanced for con-
    tingencies,
To confront night, storms, hunger, ridicule, accidents, re-
    buffs, as the trees and animals do.

# I HEAR AMERICA SINGING

I hear America singing, the varied carols I hear,
Those of mechanics, each one singing his as it should be
    blithe and strong,
The carpenter singing his as he measures his plank or beam,
The mason singing his as he makes ready for work, or leaves
    off work,
The boatman singing what belongs to him in his boat, the
    deckhand singing on the steamboat deck,

The shoemaker singing as he sits on his bench, the hatter
        singing as he stands,
The wood-cutter's song, the ploughboy's on his way in the
        morning, or at noon intermission or at sundown,
The delicious singing of the mother, or of the young wife
        at work, or of the girl sewing or washing,
Each singing what belongs to him or her and to none else,
The day what belongs to the day—at night the party of
        young fellows, robust, friendly,
Singing with open mouths their strong melodious songs.


## SHUT NOT YOUR DOORS

Shut not your doors to me proud libraries,
For that which was lacking on all your well-fill'd shelves,
        yet needed most, I bring,
Forth from the war emerging, a book I have made,
The words of my book nothing, the drift of it every thing,
A book separate, not link'd with the rest nor felt by the
        intellect,
But you ye untold latencies will thrill to every page.

# Starting From Paumanok

Starting from fish-shape Paumanok where I was born,
Well-begotten, and rais'd by a perfect mother,
After roaming many lands, lover of populous pavements,
Dweller in Mannahatta my city, or on southern savannas,
Or a soldier camp'd or carrying my knapsack and gun, or a
    miner in California,
Or rude in my home in Dakota's woods, my diet meat, my
    drink from the spring,
Or withdrawn to muse and meditate in some deep recess,
Far from the clank of crowds intervals passing rapt and
    happy,
Aware of the fresh free giver the flowing Missouri, aware
    of mighty Niagara,
Aware of the buffalo herds grazing the plains, the hirsute
    and strong-breasted bull,
Of earth, rocks, Fifth-month flowers experienced, stars,
    rain, snow, my amaze,
Having studied the mocking-bird's tones and the flight of
    the mountain-hawk,

And heard at dawn the unrivall'd one, the hermit thrush
        from the swamp-cedars,
Solitary, singing in the West, I strike up for a New World.


**2**


Victory, union, faith, identity, time,
The indissoluble compacts, riches, mystery,
Eternal progress, the kosmos, and the modern reports.


This then is life,
Here is what has come to the surface after so many throes
        and convulsions.


How curious! how real!
Underfoot the divine soil, overhead the sun.


See revolving the globe,
The ancestor-continents away group'd together,
The present and future continents north and south, with
        the isthmus between.


See, vast trackless spaces,
As in a dream they change, they swiftly fill,
Countless masses debouch upon them,
They are now cover'd with the foremost people, arts, insti-
        tutions, known.

See, projected through time,
For me an audience interminable.


With firm and regular step they wend, they never stop,
Successions of men, Americanos, a hundred millions,
One generation playing its part and passing on,
Another generation playing its part and passing on in its
       turn,
With faces turn'd sideways or backward towards me to
       listen,
With eyes retrospective towards me.


### 3

Americanos! conquerors! marches humanitarian!
Foremost! century marches! Libertad! masses!
For you a programme of chants.


Chants of the prairies,
Chants of the long-running Mississippi, and down to the
       Mexican sea,
Chants of Ohio, Indiana, Illinois, Iowa, Wisconsin and
       Minnesota,
Chants going forth from the centre from Kansas, and thence
       equi-distant,
Shooting in pulses of fire ceaseless to vivify all.

Take my leaves America, take them South and take them
      North,
Make welcome for them everywhere, for they are your own
      offspring,
Surround them East and West, for they would surround
      you,
And you precedents, connect lovingly with them, for they
      connect lovingly with you.

I conn'd old times,
I sat studying at the feet of the great masters,
Now if eligible O that the great masters might return and
      study me.

In the name of these States shall I scorn the antique?
Why these are the children of the antique to justify it.


5

Dead poets, philosophs, priests,
Martyrs, artists, inventors, governments long since,
Language-shapers on other shores,
Nations once powerful, now reduced, withdrawn, or deso-
      late,
I dare not proceed till I respectfully credit what you have
      left wafted hither,
I have perused it, own it is admirable, (moving awhile
      among it,)

9

Think nothing can ever be greater, nothing can ever deserve
       more than it deserves,
Regarding it all intently a long while, then dismissing it,
I stand in my place with my own day here.


Here lands female and male,
Here the heir-ship and heiress-ship of the world, here the
       flame of materials,
Here spirituality the translatress, the openly-avow'd,
The ever-tending, the finalè of visible forms,
The satisfier, after due long-waiting now advancing,
Yes here comes my mistress the soul.



6


The soul,
Forever and forever—longer than soil is brown and solid—
       longer than water ebbs and flows.


I will make the poems of materials, for I think they are to
       be the most spiritual poems,
And I will make the poems of my body and of mortality,
For I think I shall then supply myself with the poems of
       my soul and of immortality.


I will make a song for these States that no one State may
       under any circumstances be subjected to another
       State,

And I will make a song that there shall be comity by day
        and by night between all the States, and between any
        two of them,
And I will make a song for the ears of the President, full of
        weapons with menacing points,
And behind the weapons countless dissatisfied faces;
And a song make I of the One form'd out of all,
The fang'd and glittering One whose head is over all,
Resolute warlike One including and over all,
(However high the head of any else that head is over all.)


I will acknowledge contemporary lands,
I will trail the whole geography of the globe and salute
        courteously every city large and small,
And employments! I will put in my poems that with you is
        heroism upon land and sea,
And I will report all heroism from an American point of
        view.


I will sing the song of companionship,
I will show what alone must finally compact these,
I believe these are to found their own ideal of manly love,
        indicating it in me,
I will therefore let flame from me the burning fires that
        were threatening to consume me,
I will lift what has too long kept down those smouldering
        fires,
I will give them complete abandonment,
I will write the evangel-poem of comrades and of love,

For who but I should understand love with all its sorrow and
    joy?
And who but I should be the poet of comrades?


## 7

I am the credulous man of qualities, ages, races,
I advance from the people in their own spirit,
Here is what sings unrestricted faith.

Omnes! omnes! let others ignore what they may,
I make the poem of evil also, I commemorate that part also,
I am myself just as much evil as good, and my nation is—
    and I say there is in fact no evil,
(Or if there is I say it is just as important to you, to the land
    or to me, as any thing else.)

I too, following many and follow'd by many, inaugurate a
    religion, I descend into the arena,
(It may be I am destin'd to utter the loudest cries there, the
    winner's pealing shouts,
Who knows? they may rise from me yet, and soar above
    everything.)

Each is not for its own sake,
I say the whole earth and all the stars in the sky are for
    religion's sake.

I say no man has ever yet been half devout enough,
None has ever yet adored or worship'd half enough,

None has begun to think how divine he himself is, and how
    certain the future is.

I say that the real and permanent grandeur of these States
    must be their religion,
Otherwise there is no real and permanent grandeur;
(Nor character nor life worthy the name without religion,
Nor land nor man or woman without religion.)

## 8

What are you doing young man?
Are you so earnest, so given up to literature, science, art,
    amours?
These ostensible realities, politics, points?
Your ambition or business whatever it may be?

It is well—against such I say not a word, I am their poet
    also,
But behold! such swiftly subside, burnt up for religion's
    sake,
For not all matter is fuel to heat, impalpable flame, the
    essential life of the earth,
Any more than such are to religion.

## 9

What do you seek so pensive and silent?
What do you need camerado?
Dear son do you think it is love?

Listen dear son—listen America, daughter or son,
It is a painful thing to love a man or woman to excess, and
        yet it satisfies, it is great,
But there is something else very great, it makes the whole
        coincide,
It, magnificent, beyond materials, with continuous hands
        sweeps and provides for all.


10

Know you, solely to drop in the earth the germs of a greater
        religion,
The following chants each for its kind I sing.


My comrade!
For you to share with me two greatnesses, and a third one
        rising inclusive and more resplendent,
The greatness of Love and Democracy, and the greatness of
        Religion.


Melange mine own, the unseen and the seen,
Mysterious ocean where the streams empty,
Prophetic spirit of materials shifting and flickering around
        me,
Living beings, identities now doubtless near us in the air
        that we know not of,
Contact daily and hourly that will not release me,
These selecting, these in hints demanded of me.

Not he with a daily kiss onward from childhood kissing me,
Has winded and twisted around me that which holds me to
      him,
Any more than I am held to the heavens and all the spiritual
       world,
After what they have done to me, suggesting themes.

O such themes—equalities! O divine average!
Warblings under the sun, usher'd as now, or at noon, or set-
      ting,
Strains musical flowing through ages, now reaching hither,
I take to your reckless and composite chords, add to them,
      and cheerfully pass them forward.


## 11

As I have walk'd in Alabama my morning walk,
I have seen where the she-bird the mocking-bird sat on her
      nest in the briers hatching her brood.

I have seen the he-bird also,
I have paus'd to hear him near at hand inflating his throat
      and joyfully singing.

And while I paus'd it came to me that what he really sang
      for was not there only,
Nor for his mate nor himself only, nor all sent back by the
      echoes,

But subtle, clandestine, away beyond,
A charge transmitted and gift occult for those being born.


12

Democracy! near at hand to you a throat is now inflating it-
    self and joyfully singing.


Ma femme! for the brood beyond us and of us,
For those who belong here and those to come,
I exultant to be ready for them will now shake out carols
    stronger and haughtier than have ever yet been
    heard upon earth.


I will make the songs of passion to give them their way,
And your songs outlaw'd offenders, for I scan you with
    kindred eyes, and carry you with me the same as any.


I will make the true poem of riches,
To earn for the body and the mind whatever adheres and
    goes forward and is not dropt by death;
I will effuse egotism and show it underlying all, and I will
    be the bard of personality,
And I will show of male and female that either is but the
    equal of the other,
And sexual organs and acts! do you concentrate in me, for I
    am determin'd to tell you with courageous clear voice
    to prove you illustrious,

And I will show that there is no imperfection in the present,
        and can be none in the future,
And I will show that whatever happens to anybody it may
        be turn'd to beautiful results,
And I will show that nothing can happen more beautiful
        than death,
And I will thread a thread through my poems that time and
        events are compact,
And that all the things of the universe are perfect miracles,
        each as profound as any.


I will not make poems with reference to parts,
But I will make poems, songs, thoughts, with reference to
        ensemble,
And I will not sing with reference to a day, but with ref-
        erence to all days,
And I will not make a poem nor the least part of a poem but
        has reference to the soul,
Because having look'd at the objects of the universe, I find
        there is no one nor any particle of one but has ref-
        erence to the soul.


### 13

Was somebody asking to see the soul?
See, your own shape and countenance, persons, substances,
        beasts, the trees, the running rivers, the rocks and
        sands.

All hold spiritual joys and afterwards loosen them;
How can the real body ever die and be buried?

Of your real body and any man's or woman's real body,
Item for item it will elude the hands of the corpse-cleaners
        and pass to fitting spheres,
Carrying what has accrued to it from the moment of birth to
        the moment of death.

Not the types set up by the printer return their impression,
        the meaning, the main concern,
Any more than a man's substance and life or a woman's
        substance and life return in the body and the soul,
Indifferently before death and after death.

Behold, the body includes and is the meaning, the main
        concern, and includes and is the soul;
Whoever you are, how superb and how divine is your body,
        or any part of it!

14

Whoever you are, to you endless announcements!

Daughter of the lands did you wait for your poet?
Did you wait for one with a flowing mouth and indicative
        hand?

Toward the male of the States, and toward the female of
    the States,
Exulting words, words to Democracy's lands.


Interlink'd, food-yielding lands!
Land of coal and iron! land of gold! land of cotton, sugar,
    rice!
Land of wheat, beef, pork! land of wool and hemp! land of
    the apple and the grape!
Land of the pastoral plains, the grass-fields of the world!
    land of those sweet-air'd interminable plateaus!
Land of the herd, the garden, the healthy house of adobie!
Lands where the north-west Columbia winds, and where
    the south-west Colorado winds!
Land of the eastern Chesapeake! land of the Delaware!
Land of Ontario, Erie, Huron, Michigan!
Land of the Old Thirteen! Massachusetts land! land of
    Vermont and Connecticut!
Land of the ocean shores! land of sierras and peaks!
Land of boatmen and sailors! fishermen's land!
Inextricable lands! the clutch'd together! the passionate
    ones!
The side by side! the elder and younger brothers! the bony-
    limb'd!
The great women's land! the feminine! the experienced
    sisters and the inexperienced sisters!
Far breath'd land! Arctic braced! Mexican breez'd! the
    diverse! the compact!
The Pennsylvanian! the Virginian! the double Carolinian!

O all and each well-loved by me! my intrepid nations! O I at
  any rate include you all with perfect love!
I cannot be discharged from you! not from one any sooner
  than another!
O death! O for all that, I am yet of you unseen this hour with
  irrepressible love,
Walking New England, a friend, a traveler,
Splashing my bare feet in the edge of the summer ripples on
  Paumanok's sands,
Crossing the prairies, dwelling again in Chicago, dwelling
  in every town,
Observing shows, births, improvements, structures, arts,
Listening to orators and oratresses in public halls,
Of and through the States as during life, each man and
  woman my neighbor,
The Louisianian, the Georgian, as near to me, and I as near
  to him and her,
The Mississippian and Arkansian yet with me, and I yet
  with any of them,
Yet upon the plains west of the spinal river, yet in my house
  of adobie,
Yet returning eastward, yet in the Seaside State or in Mary-
  land,
Yet Kanadian cheerily braving the winter, the snow and ice
  welcome to me,
Yet a true son either of Maine or of the Granite State, or
  the Narragansett Bay State, or the Empire State,
Yet sailing to other shores to annex the same, yet welcoming
  every new brother,

Hereby applying these leaves to the new ones from the hour
        they unite with the old ones,
Coming among the new ones myself to be their companion
        and equal, coming personally to you now,
Enjoining you to acts, characters, spectacles, with me.


## 15

With me with firm holding, yet haste, haste on.

For your life adhere to me,
(I may have to be persuaded many times before I consent to
        give myself really to you, but what of that?
Must not Nature be persuaded many times?)

No dainty dolce affettuoso I,
Bearded, sun-burnt, gray-neck'd, forbidding, I have arrived,
To be wrestled with as I pass for the solid prizes of the uni-
        verse,
For such I afford whoever can persevere to win them.


## 16

On my way a moment I pause,
Here for you! and here for America!
Still the present I raise aloft, still the future of the States I
        harbinge glad and sublime,
And for the past I pronounce what the air holds of the red
        aborigines.

The red aborigines,

Leaving natural breaths, sounds of rain and winds, calls as
of birds and animals in the woods, syllabled to us
for names,

Okonee, Koosa, Ottawa, Monongahela, Sauk, Natchez,
Chattahoochee, Kaqueta, Oronoco,

Wabash, Miami, Saginaw, Chippewa, Oshkosh, Walla-
Walla,

Leaving such to the States they melt, they depart, charging
the water and the land with names.

## 17

Expanding and swift, henceforth,

Elements, breeds, adjustments, turbulent, quick and au-
dacious,

A world primal again, vistas of glory incessant and branch-
ing,

A new race dominating previous ones and grander far, with
new contests,

New politics, new literatures and religions, new inventions
and arts.


These, my voice announcing—I will sleep no more but
arise,

You oceans that have been calm within me! how I feel you,
fathomless, stirring, preparing unprecedented waves
and storms.

See, steamers steaming through my poems,

See, in my poems immigrants continually coming and land-
ing,

See, in arriere, the wigwam, the trail, the hunter's hut, the
flat-boat, the maize-leaf, the claim, the rude fence,
and the backwoods village,

See, on the one side the Western Sea and on the other the
Eastern Sea, how they advance and retreat upon my
poems as upon their own shores,

See, pastures and forests in my poems—see, animals wild
and tame—see, beyond the Kaw, countless herds of
buffalo feeding on short curly grass,

See, in my poems, cities, solid, vast, inland, with paved
streets, with iron and stone edifices, ceaseless
vehicles, and commerce,

See, the many-cylinder'd steam printing-press—see, the
electric telegraph stretching across the continent,

See, through Atlantica's depths pulses American Europe
reaching, pulses of Europe duly return'd,

See, the strong and quick locomotive as it departs, panting,
blowing the steam-whistle,

See, ploughmen ploughing farms—see, miners digging
mines—see, the numberless factories,

See, mechanics busy at their benches with tools—see from
among them superior judges, philosophs, Presi-
dents, emerge, drest in working dresses,

See, lounging through the shops and fields of the States, me
    well-belov'd, close-held by day and night,
Hear the loud echoes of my songs there—read the hints
    come at last.

## 19

O camerado close! O you and me at last, and us two only.
O a word to clear one's path ahead endlessly!
O something ecstatic and undemonstrable! O music wild!
O now I triumph—and you shall also;
O hand in hand—O wholesome pleasure—O one more de-
    sirer and lover!
O to haste firm holding—to haste, haste on with me.

# Song of Myself

## I

I celebrate myself, and sing myself,
And what I assume you shall assume,
For every atom belonging to me as good belongs to you.

I loafe and invite my soul,
I lean and loafe at my ease observing a spear of summer
    grass.

My tongue, every atom of my blood, form'd from this soil,
    this air,
Born here of parents born here from parents the same, and
    their parents the same,
I, now thirty-seven years old in perfect health begin,
Hoping to cease not till death.

Creeds and schools in abeyance,
Retiring back a while sufficed at what they are, but never
    forgotten,
I harbor for good or bad, I permit to speak at every hazard,
Nature without check with original energy.

## 2

Houses and rooms are full of perfumes, the shelves are
 crowded with perfumes,
I breathe the fragrance myself and know it and like it,
The distillation would intoxicate me also, but I shall not
 let it.

The atmosphere is not a perfume, it has no taste of the dis-
 tillation, it is odorless,
It is for my mouth forever, I am in love with it,
I will go to the bank by the wood and become undisguised
 and naked,
I am mad for it to be in contact with me.

The smoke of my own breath,
Echoes, ripples, buzz'd whispers, love-root, silk-thread,
 crotch and vine,
My respiration and inspiration, the beating of my heart,
 the passing of blood and air through my lungs,
The sniff of green leaves and dry leaves, and of the shore
 and dark-color'd sea-rocks, and of hay in the barn,
The sound of the belch'd words of my voice loos'd to the
 eddies of the wind,
A few light kisses, a few embraces, a reaching around of
 arms,
The play of shine and shade on the trees as the supple
 boughs wag,
The delight alone or in the rush of the streets, or along the
 fields and hill-sides,

The feeling of health, the full-noon trill, the song of me
        rising from bed and meeting the sun.

Have you reckon'd a thousand acres much? have you
        reckon'd the earth much?
Have you practis'd so long to learn to read?
Have you felt so proud to get at the meaning of poems?

Stop this day and night with me and you shall possess the
        origin of all poems,
You shall possess the good of the earth and sun, (there are
        millions of suns left,)
You shall no longer take things at second or third hand, nor
        look through the eyes of the dead, nor feed on the
        spectres in books,
You shall not look through my eyes either, nor take things
        from me,
You shall listen to all sides and filter them from your self.

### 3

I have heard what the talkers were talking, the talk of the
        beginning and the end,
But I do not talk of the beginning or the end.

There was never any more inception than there is now,
Nor any more youth or age than there is now,
And will never be any more perfection than there is now,
Nor any more heaven or hell than there is now.

Urge and urge and urge,
Always the procreant urge of the world.
Out of the dimness opposite equals advance, always substance and increase, always sex,
Always a knit of identity, always distinction, always a breed of life.

To elaborate is no avail, learn'd and unlearn'd feel that it is so.

Sure as the most certain sure, plumb in the uprights, well entretied, braced in the beams,
Stout as a horse, affectionate, haughty, electrical,
I and this mystery here we stand.

Clear and sweet is my soul, and clear and sweet is all that is not my soul.

Lack one lacks both, and the unseen is proved by the seen,
Till that becomes unseen and receives proof in its turn.

Showing the best and dividing it from the worst age vexes age,
Knowing the perfect fitness and equanimity of things, while they discuss I am silent, and go bathe and admire myself.

Welcome is every organ and attribute of me, and of any man hearty and clean,

Not an inch nor a particle of an inch is vile, and none shall
      be less familiar than the rest.


I am satisfied—I see, dance, laugh, sing;
As the hugging and loving bed-fellow sleeps at my side
      through the night, and withdraws at the peep of the
      day with stealthy tread,
Leaving me baskets cover'd with white towels swelling the
      house with their plenty,
Shall I postpone my acceptation and realization and scream
      at my eyes,
That they turn from gazing after and down the road,
And forthwith cipher and show me to a cent,
Exactly the value of one and exactly the value of two, and
      which is ahead?



4


Trippers and askers surround me,
People I meet, the effect upon me of my early life or the
      ward and city I live in, or the nation,
The latest dates, discoveries, inventions, societies, authors
      old and new,
My dinner, dress, associates, looks, compliments, dues,
The real or fancied indifference of some man or woman I
      love,
The sickness of one of my folks or of myself, or ill-doing or
      loss or lack of money, or depressions or exaltations,

Battles, the horrors of fratricidal war, the fever of doubtful
news, the fitful events;
These come to me days and nights and go from me again,
But they are not the Me myself.

Apart from the pulling and hauling stands what I am,
Stands amused, complacent, compassionating, idle, unitary,
Looks down, is erect, or bends an arm on an impalpable cer-
tain rest,
Looking with side-curved head curious what will come next,
Both in and out of the game and watching and wondering
at it.

Backward I see in my own days where I sweated through
fog with linguists and contenders,
I have no mockings or arguments, I witness and wait.


5

I believe in you my soul, the other I am must not abase itself
to you,
And you must not be abased to the other.

Loafe with me on the grass, loose the stop from your throat,
Not words, not music or rhyme I want, not custom or lec-
ture, not even the best,
Only the lull I like, the hum of your valvèd voice.

I mind how once we lay such a transparent summer morning,
How you settled your head athwart my hips and gently
      turn'd over upon me,
And parted the shirt from my bosom-bone, and plunged
      your tongue to my bare-stript heart,
And reach'd till you felt my beard, and reach'd till you held
      my feet.

Swiftly arose and spread around me the peace and knowl-
      edge that pass all the argument of the earth,
And I know that the hand of God is the promise of my own,
And I know that the spirit of God is the brother of my own,
And that all the men ever born are also my brothers, and
      the women my sisters and lovers,
And that a kelson of the creation is love,
And limitless are leaves stiff or drooping in the fields,
And brown ants in the little wells beneath them,
And mossy scabs of the worm fence, heap'd stones, elder,
      mullein and poke-weed.


### 6

A child said *What is the grass?* fetching it to me with full
      hands;
How could I answer the child? I do not know what it is any
      more than he.

I guess it must be the flag of my disposition, out of hopeful
      green stuff woven.

Or I guess it is the handkerchief of the Lord,
A scented gift and remembrancer designedly dropt,
Bearing the owner's name someway in the corners, that we
may see and remark, and say *Whose?*


Or I guess the grass is itself a child, the produced babe of
the vegetation.


Or I guess it is a uniform hieroglyphic,
And it means, Sprouting alike in broad zones and narrow
zones,
Growing among black folks as among white,
Kanuck, Tuckahoe, Congressman, Cuff, I give them the
same, I receive them the same.


And now it seems to me the beautiful uncut hair of graves.


Tenderly will I use you curling grass,
It may be you transpire from the breasts of young men,
It may be if I had known them I would have loved them,
It may be you are from old people, or from offspring taken
soon out of their mothers' laps,
And here you are the mothers' laps.


This grass is very dark to be from the white heads of old
mothers,
Darker than the colorless beards of old men,
Dark to come from under the faint red roofs of mouths.

O I perceive after all so many uttering tongues,
And I perceive they do not come from the roofs of mouths
    for nothing.


I wish I could translate the hints about the dead young men
    and women,
And the hints about old men and mothers, and the offspring
    taken soon out of their laps.


What do you think has become of the young and old men?
And what do you think has become of the women and chil-
    dren?


They are alive and well somewhere,
The smallest sprout shows there is really no death,
And if ever there was it led forward life, and does not wait
    at the end to arrest it,
And ceas'd the moment life appear'd.


All goes onward and outward, nothing collapses,
And to die is different from what any one supposed, and
    luckier.


### 7

Has any one supposed it lucky to be born?
I hasten to inform him or her it is just as lucky to die, and I
    know it.

I pass death with the dying and birth with the new-wash'd
     babe, and am not contain'd between my hat and
     boots,
And peruse manifold objects, no two alike and every one
     good,
The earth good and the stars good, and their adjuncts all
     good.


I am not an earth nor an adjunct of an earth,
I am the mate and companion of people, all just as im-
     mortal and fathomless as myself,
(They do not know how immortal, but I know.)


Every kind for itself and its own, for me mine male and
     female,
For me those that have been boys and that love women,
For me the man that is proud and feels how it stings to be
     slighted,
For me the sweet-heart and the old maid, for me mothers
     and the mothers of mothers,
For me lips that have smiled, eyes that have shed tears,
For me children and the begetters of children.


Undrape! you are not guilty to me, nor stale nor discarded,
I see through the broadcloth and gingham whether or no,
And am around, tenacious, acquisitive, tireless, and cannot
     be shaken away.

The little one sleeps in its cradle,
I lift the gauze and look a long time, and silently brush away
flies with my hand.


The youngster and the red-faced girl turn aside up the bushy
        hill,
I peeringly view them from the top.


The suicide sprawls on the bloody floor of the bedroom,
I witness the corpse with its dabbled hair, I note where the
        pistol has fallen.


The blab of the pave, tires of carts, sluff of boot-soles, talk
        of the promenaders,
The heavy omnibus, the driver with his interrogating
        thumb, the clank of the shod horses on the granite
        floor,
The snow-sleighs, clinking, shouted jokes, pelts of snow-
        balls,
The hurrahs for popular favorites, the fury of rous'd mobs,
The flap of the curtain'd litter, a sick man inside borne to
        the hospital,
The meeting of enemies, the sudden oath, the blows and
        fall,
The excited crowd, the policeman with his star quickly
        working his passage to the centre of the crowd,
The impassive stones that receive and return so many echoes,

What groans of over-fed or half-starv'd who fall sunstruck
      or in fits,
What exclamations of women taken suddenly who hurry
      home and give birth to babes,
What living and buried speech is always vibrating here,
      what howls restrain'd by decorum,
Arrests of criminals, slights, adulterous offers made, ac-
      ceptances, rejections with convex lips,
I mind them or the show or resonance of them—I come and
      I depart.


## 9

The big doors of the country barn stand open and ready,
The dried grass of the harvest-time loads the slow-drawn
      wagon,
The clear light plays on the brown gray and green inter-
      tinged,
The armfuls are pack'd to the sagging mow.


I am there, I help, I came stretch'd atop of the load,
I felt its soft jolts, one leg reclined on the other,
I jump from the cross-beams and seize the clover and
      timothy,
And roll head over heels and tangle my hair full of wisps.

## 10

Alone far in the wilds and mountains I hunt,
Wandering amazed at my own lightness and glee,
In the late afternoon choosing a safe spot to pass the night,
Kindling a fire and broiling the fresh-kill'd game,
Falling asleep on the gather'd leaves with my dog and gun
        by my side.


The Yankee clipper is under her sky-sails, she cuts the
        sparkle and scud,
My eyes settle the land, I bend at her prow or shout joyously
        from the deck.


The boatmen and clam-diggers arose early and stopt for me,
I tuck'd my trowser-ends in my boots and went and had a
        good time;
You should have been with us that day round the chowder-
        kettle.


I saw the marriage of the trapper in the open air in the far
        west, the bride was a red girl,
Her father and his friends sat near cross-legged and dumbly
        smoking, they had moccasins to their feet and large
        thick blankets hanging from their shoulders,
On a bank lounged the trapper, he was drest mostly in skins,
        his luxuriant beard and curls protected his neck, he
        held his bride by the hand,

She had long eyelashes, her head was bare, her coarse
    straight locks descended upon her voluptuous limbs
    and reach'd to her feet.


The runaway slave came to my house and stopt outside,
I heard his motions crackling the twigs of the woodpile,
Through the swung half-door of the kitchen I saw him
    limpsy and weak,
And went where he sat on a log and led him in and assured
    him,
And brought water and fill'd a tub for his sweated body
    and bruis'd feet,
And gave him a room that enter'd from my own, and gave
    him some coarse clean clothes,
And remember perfectly well his revolving eyes and his
    awkwardness,
And remember putting plasters on the galls of his neck and
    ankles;
He staid with me a week before he was recuperated and
    pass'd north,
I had him sit next me at table, my fire-lock lean'd in the
    corner.


11

Twenty-eight young men bathe by the shore,
Twenty-eight young men and all so friendly;
Twenty-eight years of womanly life and all so lonesome.

She owns the fine house by the rise of the bank,
She hides handsome and richly drest aft the blinds of the
          window.


Which of the young men does she like the best?
Ah the homeliest of them is beautiful to her.


Where are you off to, lady? for I see you,
You splash in the water there, yet stay stock still in your
          room.


Dancing and laughing along the beach came the twenty-
          ninth bather,
The rest did not see her, but she saw them and loved them.


The beards of the young men glisten'd with wet, it ran from
          their long hair,
Little streams pass'd all over their bodies.


An unseen hand also pass'd over their bodies,
It descended tremblingly from their temples and ribs.


The young men float on their backs, their white bellies bulge
          to the sun, they do not ask who seizes fast to them,
They do not know who puffs and declines with pendant and
          bending arch,
They do not think whom they souse with spray.

## 12

The butcher-boy puts off his killing-clothes, or sharpens his
  knife at the stall in the market,
I loiter enjoying his repartee and his shuffle and break-down.


Blacksmiths with grimed and hairy chests environ the anvil,
Each has his main-sledge, they are all out, there is a great
  heat in the fire.


From the cinder-strew'd threshold I follow their move-
  ments,
The lithe sheer of their waists plays even with their massive
  arms,
Overhand the hammers swing, overhand so slow, overhand
  so sure,
They do not hasten, each man hits in his place.

## 13

The negro holds firmly the reins of his four horses, the
  block swags underneath on its tied-over chain,
The negro that drives the long dray of the stone-yard, steady
  and tall he stands pois'd on one leg on the string-
  piece,
His blue shirt exposes his ample neck and breast and loosens
  over his hip-band,
His glance is calm and commanding, he tosses the slouch of
  his hat away from his forehead,

The sun falls on his crispy hair and mustache, falls on the
  black of his polish'd and perfect limbs.

I behold the picturesque giant and love him, and I do not
  stop there,
I go with the team also.

In me the caresser of life wherever moving, backward as
  well as forward sluing,
To niches aside and junior bending, not a person or object
  missing,
Absorbing all to myself and for this song.

Oxen that rattle the yoke and chain or halt in the leafy shade,
  what is that you express in your eyes?
It seems to me more than all the print I have read in my life.

My tread scares the wood-drake and wood-duck on my dis-
  tant and day-long ramble,
They rise together, they slowly circle around.

I believe in those wing'd purposes,
And acknowledge red, yellow, white, playing within me,
And consider green and violet and the tufted crown inten-
  tional,
And do not call the tortoise unworthy because she is not
  something else,
And the jay in the woods never studied the gamut, yet trills
  pretty well to me,
And the look of the bay mare shames silliness out of me.

The wild gander leads his flock through the cool night,
*Ya-honk* he says, and sounds it down to me like an invitation,
The pert may suppose it meaningless, but I listening close,
Find its purpose and place up there toward the wintry sky.


The sharp-hoof'd moose of the north, the cat on the house-sill, the chickadee, the prairie-dog,
The litter of the grunting sow as they tug at her teats,
The brood of the turkey-hen and she with her half-spread wings,
I see in them and myself the same old law.


The press of my foot to the earth springs a hundred affections,
They scorn the best I can do to relate them.


I am enamour'd of growing out-doors,
Of men that live among cattle or taste of the ocean or woods,
Of the builders and steerers of ships and the wielders of axes and mauls, and the drivers of horses,
I can eat and sleep with them week in and week out.


What is commonest, cheapest, nearest, easiest, is Me,
Me going in for my chances, spending for vast returns,
Adorning myself to bestow myself on the first that will take me,

Not asking the sky to come down to my good will,
Scattering it freely forever.

The pure contralto sings in the organ loft,
The carpenter dresses his plank, the tongue of his foreplane
     whistles its wild ascending lisp,
The married and unmarried children ride home to their
     Thanksgiving dinner,
The pilot seizes the king-pin, he heaves down with a strong
     arm,
The mate stands braced in the whale-boat, lance and
     harpoon are ready,
The duck-shooter walks by silent and cautious stretches,
The deacons are ordain'd with cross'd hands at the altar,
The spinning-girl retreats and advances to the hum of the
     big wheel,
The farmer stops by the bars as he walks on a First-day loafe
     and looks at the oats and rye,
The lunatic is carried at last to the asylum a confirm'd case,
(He will never sleep any more as he did in the cot in his
     mother's bed-room;)
The jour printer with gray head and gaunt jaws works at his
     case,
He turns his quid of tobacco while his eyes blurr with the
     manuscript;
The malform'd limbs are tied to the surgeon's table,

What is removed drops horribly in a pail;

The quadroon girl is sold at the auction-stand, the drunkard
        nods by the bar-room stove,

The machinist rolls up his sleeves, the policeman travels his
        beat, the gate-keeper marks who pass,

The young fellow drives the express-wagon, (I love him,
        though I do not know him;)

The half-breed straps on his light boots to compete in the
        race,

The western turkey-shooting draws old and young, some
        lean on their rifles, some sit on logs,

Out from the crowd steps the marksman, takes his position,
        levels his piece;

The groups of newly-come immigrants cover the wharf or
        levee,

As the woolly-pates hoe in the sugar-field, the overseer views
        them from his saddle,

The bugle calls in the ball-room, the gentlemen run for
        their partners, the dancers bow to each other,

The youth lies awake in the cedar-roof'd garret and harks to
        the musical rain,

The Wolverine sets traps on the creek that helps fill the
        Huron,

The squaw wrapt in her yellow-hemm'd cloth is offering
        moccasins and bead-bags for sale,

The connoisseur peers along the exhibition-gallery with
        half-shut eyes bent sideways,

As the deck-hands make fast the steamboat the plank is
        thrown for the shore-going passengers,

The young sister holds out the skein while the elder sister
        winds it off in a ball, and stops now and then for the
        knots,
The one-year wife is recovering and happy having a week
        ago borne her first child,
The clean-hair'd Yankee girl works with her sewing-ma-
        chine or in the factory or mill,
The paving-man leans on his two-handed rammer, the re-
        porter's lead flies swiftly over the note-book, the
        sign-painter is lettering with blue and gold,
The canal boy trots on the tow-path, the book-keeper counts
        at his desk, the shoemaker waxes his thread,
The conductor beats time for the band and all the perform-
        ers follow him,
The child is baptized, the convert is making his first pro-
        fessions,
The regatta is spread on the bay, the race is begun, (how
        the white sails sparkle!)
The drover watching his drove sings out to them that would
        stray,
The pedler sweats with his pack on his back, (the purchaser
        higgling about the odd cent;)
The bride unrumples her white dress, the minute-hand of
        the clock moves slowly,
The opium-eater reclines with rigid head and just-open'd
        lips,
The prostitute draggles her shawl, her bonnet bobs on her
        tipsy and pimpled neck,
The crowd laugh at her blackguard oaths, the men jeer and
        wink to each other,

(Miserable! I do not laugh at your oaths nor jeer you;)

The President holding a cabinet council is surrounded by the great Secretaries,

On the piazza walk three matrons stately and friendly with twined arms,

The crew of the fish-smack pack repeated layers of halibut in the hold,

The Missourian crosses the plains toting his wares and his cattle,

As the fare-collector goes through the train he gives notice by the jingling of loose change,

The floor-men are laying the floor, the tinners are tinning the roof, the masons are calling for mortar,

In single file each shouldering his hod pass onward the laborers;

Seasons pursuing each other the indescribable crowd is gather'd, it is the fourth of Seventh-month, (what salutes of cannon and small arms!)

Seasons pursuing each other the plougher ploughs, the mower mows, and the winter-grain falls in the ground;

Off on the lakes the pike-fisher watches and waits by the hole in the frozen surface,

The stumps stand thick round the clearing, the squatter strikes deep with his axe,

Flatboatmen make fast towards dusk near the cotton-wood or pecan-trees,

Coon-seekers go through the regions of the Red river or through those drain'd by the Tennessee, or through those of the Arkansas,

Torches shine in the dark that hangs on the Chattahooche
        or Altamahaw,
Patriarchs sit at supper with sons and grandsons and great-
        grandsons around them,
In walls of adobie, in canvas tents, rest hunters and trappers
        after their day's sport,
The city sleeps and the country sleeps,
The living sleep for their time, the dead sleep for their time,
The old husband sleeps by his wife and the young husband
        sleeps by his wife;
And these tend inward to me, and I tend outward to them,
And such as it is to be of these more or less I am,
And of these one and all I weave the song of myself.


16

I am of old and young, of the foolish as much as the wise,
Regardless of others, ever regardful of others,
Maternal as well as paternal, a child as well as a man,
Stuff'd with the stuff that is coarse and stuff'd with the stuff
        that is fine,
One of the Nation of many nations, the smallest the same
        and the largest the same,
A Southerner soon as a Northerner, a planter nonchalant
        and hospitable down by the Oconee I live,
A Yankee bound my own way ready for trade, my joints the
        limberest joints on earth and the sternest joints on
        earth,

A Kentuckian walking the vale of the Elkhorn in my deer-
skin leggings, a Louisianian or Georgian,
A boatman over lakes or bays or along coasts, a Hoosier,
Badger, Buckeye;
At home on Kanadian snow-shoes or up in the bush, or
with fishermen off Newfoundland,
At home in the fleet of ice-boats, sailing with the rest and
tacking,
At home on the hills of Vermont or in the woods of Maine,
or the Texan ranch,
Comrade of Californians, comrade of free North-Western-
ers, (loving their big proportions,)
Comrade of raftsmen and coalmen, comrade of all who
shake hands and welcome to drink and meat,
A learner with the simplest, a teacher of the thoughtfullest,
A novice beginning yet experient of myriads of seasons,
Of every hue and caste am I, of every rank and religion,
A farmer, mechanic, artist, gentleman, sailor, quaker,
Prisoner, fancy-man, rowdy, lawyer, physician, priest.


I resist any thing better than my own diversity,
Breathe the air but leave plenty after me,
And am not stuck up, and am in my place.


(The moth and the fish-eggs are in their place,
The bright suns I see and the dark suns I cannot see are in
their place,
The palpable is in its place and the impalpable is in its
place.)

## 17

These are really the thoughts of all men in all ages and lands,
    they are not original with me,
If they are not yours as much as mine they are nothing, or
    next to nothing,
If they are not the riddle and the untying of the riddle they
    are nothing,
If they are not just as close as they are distant they are
    nothing.


This is the grass that grows wherever the land is and the
    water is,
This the common air that bathes the globe.

## 18

With music strong I come, with my cornets and my drums,
I play not marches for accepted victors only, I play marches
    for conquer'd and slain persons.


Have you heard that it was good to gain the day?
I also say it is good to fall, battles are lost in the same spirit
    in which they are won.


I beat and pound for the dead,
I blow through my embouchures my loudest and gayest for
    them.

Vivas to those who have fail'd!
And to those whose war-vessels sank in the sea!
And to those themselves who sank in the sea!
And to all generals that lost engagements, and all overcome
heroes!
And the numberless unknown heroes equal to the greatest
heroes known!


19

This is the meal equally set, this the meat for natural hunger,
It is for the wicked just the same as the righteous, I make
appointments with all,
I will not have a single person slighted or left away,
The kept-woman, sponger, thief, are hereby invited,
The heavy-lipp'd slave is invited, the venerealee is invited;
There shall be no difference between them and the rest.


This is the press of a bashful hand, this the float and odor of
hair,
This the touch of my lips to yours, this the murmur of
yearning,
This the far-off depth and height reflecting my own face,
This the thoughtful merge of myself, and the outlet again.


Do you guess I have some intricate purpose?
Well I have, for the Fourth-month showers have, and the
mica on the side of a rock has.

Do you take it I would astonish?
Does the daylight astonish? does the early redstart twittering
        through the woods?
Do I astonish more than they?

This hour I tell things in confidence,
I might not tell everybody, but I will tell you.


### 20

Who goes there? hankering, gross, mystical, nude;
How is it I extract strength from the beef I eat?

What is a man anyhow? what am I? what are you?

All I mark as my own you shall offset it with your own,
Else it were time lost listening to me.

I do not snivel that snivel the world over,
That months are vacuums and the ground but wallow and
        filth.

Whimpering and truckling fold with powders for invalids,
        conformity goes to the fourth-remov'd,
I wear my hat as I please indoors or out.

Why should I pray? why should I venerate and be ceremoni-
        ous?

Having pried through the strata, analyzed to a hair, counsel'd with doctors and calculated close,
I find no sweeter fat than sticks to my own bones.

In all people I see myself, none more and not one a barley-corn less,
And the good or bad I say of myself I say of them.

I know I am solid and sound,
To me the converging objects of the universe perpetually flow,
All are written to me, and I must get what the writing means.

I know I am deathless,
I know this orbit of mine cannot be swept by a carpenter's compass,
I know I shall not pass like a child's carlacue cut with a burnt stick at night.

I know I am august,
I do not trouble my spirit to vindicate itself or be understood,
I see that the elementary laws never apologize,
(I reckon I behave no prouder than the level I plant my house by, after all.)

I exist as I am, that is enough,
If no other in the world be aware I sit content,
And if each and all be aware I sit content.

One world is aware and by far the largest to me, and that is
    myself,
And whether I come to my own to-day or in ten thousand or
    ten million years,
I can cheerfully take it now, or with equal cheerfulness I can
    wait.

My foothold is tenon'd and mortis'd in granite,
I laugh at what you call dissolution,
And I know the amplitude of time.

### 21

I am the poet of the Body and I am the poet of the Soul,
The pleasures of heaven are with me and the pains of hell
    are with me,
The first I graft and increase upon myself, the latter I trans-
    late into a new tongue.

I am the poet of the woman the same as the man,
And I say it is as great to be a woman as to be a man,
And I say there is nothing greater than the mother of men.

I chant the chant of dilation or pride,
We have had ducking and deprecating about enough,
I show that size is only development.

Have you outstript the rest? are you the President?
It is a trifle, they will more than arrive there every one, and
    still pass on.

I am he that walks with the tender and growing night,
I call to the earth and sea half-held by the night.
Press close bare-bosom'd night—press close magnetic
     nourishing night!
Night of south winds—night of the large few stars!
Still nodding night—mad naked summer night.

Smile O voluptuous cool-breath'd earth!
Earth of the slumbering and liquid trees!
Earth of departed sunset—earth of the mountains misty-
     topt!
Earth of the vitreous pour of the full moon just tinged with
     blue!
Earth of shine and dark mottling the tide of the river!
Earth of the limpid gray of clouds brighter and clearer for
     my sake!
Far-swooping elbow'd earth—rich apple-blossom'd earth!
Smile, for your lover comes.

Prodigal, you have given me love—therefore I to you give
     love!
O unspeakable passionate love.

22

You sea! I resign myself to you also—I guess what you
     mean,
I behold from the beach your crooked inviting fingers,
I believe you refuse to go back without feeling of me,

54

We must have a turn together, I undress, hurry me out of
      sight of the land,
Cushion me soft, rock me in billowy drowse,
Dash me with amorous wet, I can repay you.


Sea of stretch'd ground-swells,
Sea breathing broad and convulsive breaths,
Sea of the brine of life and of unshovell'd yet always-
      ready graves,
Howler and scooper of storms, capricious and dainty sea,
I am integral with you, I too am of one phase and of all
      phases.


Partaker of influx and efflux I, extoller of hate and con-
      ciliation,
Extoller of amies and those that sleep in each others' arms.


I am he attesting sympathy,
(Shall I make my list of things in the house and skip the
      house that supports them?)


I am not the poet of goodness only, I do not decline to be
      the poet of wickedness also.


What blurt is this about virtue and about vice?
Evil propels me and reform of evil propels me, I stand
      indifferent,
My gait is no fault-finder's or rejecter's gait,
I moisten the roots of all that has grown.

Did you fear some scrofula out of the unflagging pregnancy?
Did you guess the celestial laws are yet to be work'd over
      and rectified?

I find one side a balance and the antipodal side a balance,
Soft doctrine as steady help as stable doctrine,
Thoughts and deeds of the present our rouse and early
      start.

This minute that comes to me over the past decillions,
There is no better than it and now.

What behaved well in the past or behaves well to-day is
      not such a wonder,
The wonder is always and always how there can be a mean
      man or an infidel.

## 23

Endless unfolding of words of ages!
And mine a word of the modern, the word En-Masse.

A word of the faith that never balks,
Here or henceforward it is all the same to me, I accept Time
      absolutely.

It alone is without flaw, it alone rounds and completes all,
That mystic baffling wonder alone completes all.

I accept Reality and dare not question it,
Materialism first and last imbuing.

Hurrah for positive science! long live exact demonstration!
Fetch stonecrop mixt with cedar and branches of lilac,
This is the lexicographer, this the chemist, this made a gram-
        mar of the old cartouches,
These mariners put the ship through dangerous unknown
        seas,
This is the geologist, this works with the scalpel, and this
        is a mathematician.

Gentlemen, to you the first honors always!
Your facts are useful, and yet they are not my dwelling,
I but enter by them to an area of my dwelling.

Less the reminders of properties told my words,
And more the reminders they of life untold, and of freedom
        and extrication,
And make short account of neuters and geldings, and favor
        men and women fully equipt,
And beat the gong of revolt, and stop with fugitives and
        them that plot and conspire.


24

Walt Whitman, a kosmos, of Manhattan the son,
Turbulent, fleshy, sensual, eating, drinking and breeding,
No sentimentalist, no stander above men and women or
        apart from them,
No more modest than immodest.

57

Unscrew the locks from the doors!
Unscrew the doors themselves from their jambs!

Whoever degrades another degrades me,
And whatever is done or said returns at last to me.

Through me the afflatus surging and surging, through me
the current and index.

I speak the pass-word primeval, I give the sign of democracy,
By God! I will accept nothing which all cannot have their
counterpart of on the same terms.

Through me many long dumb voices,
Voices of the interminable generations of prisoners and
slaves,
Voices of the diseas'd and despairing and of thieves and
dwarfs,
Voices of cycles of preparation and accretion,
And of the threads that connect the stars, and of wombs
and of the father-stuff,
And of the rights of them the others are down upon,
Of the deform'd, trivial, flat, foolish, despised,
Fog in the air, beetles rolling balls of dung.

Through me forbidden voices,
Voices of sexes and lusts, voices veil'd and I remove the veil,
Voices indecent by me clarified and transfigur'd.

I do not press my fingers across my mouth,
I keep as delicate around the bowels as around the head and
        heart,
Copulation is no more rank to me than death is.


I believe in the flesh and the appetites,
Seeing, hearing, feeling, are miracles, and each part and
        tag of me is a miracle.


Divine am I inside and out, and I make holy whatever I
        touch or am touch'd from,
The scent of these arm-pits aroma finer than prayer,
This head more than churches, bibles, and all the creeds.


If I worship one thing more than another it shall be the
        spread of my own body, or any part of it,
Translucent mould of me it shall be you!
Shaded ledges and rests it shall be you!
Firm masculine colter it shall be you!
Whatever goes to the tilth of me it shall be you!
You my rich blood! your milky stream pale strippings of my
        life!
Breast that presses against other breasts it shall be you!
My brain it shall be your occult convolutions!
Root of wash'd sweet-flag! timorous pond-snipe! nest of
        guarded duplicate eggs! it shall be you!
Mix'd tussled hay of head, beard, brawn, it shall be you!
Trickling sap of maple, fibre of manly wheat, it shall be
        you!

Sun so generous it shall be you!
Vapors lighting and shading my face it shall be you!
You sweaty brooks and dews it shall be you!
Winds whose soft-tickling genitals rub against me it shall
      be you!
Broad muscular fields, branches of live oak, loving lounger
      in my winding paths, it shall be you!
Hands I have taken, face I have kiss'd, mortal I have ever
      touch'd, it shall be you.


I dote on myself, there is that lot of me and all so luscious,
Each moment and whatever happens thrills me with joy,
I cannot tell how my ankles bend, nor whence the cause of
      my faintest wish,
Nor the cause of the friendship I emit, nor the cause of the
      friendship I take again.


That I walk up my stoop, I pause to consider if it really be,
A morning-glory at my window satisfies me more than the
      metaphysics of books.


To behold the day-break!
The little light fades the immense and diaphanous shadows,
The air tastes good to my palate.


Hefts of the moving world at innocent gambols silently
      rising freshly exuding,
Scooting obliquely high and low.

Something I cannot see puts upward libidinous prongs,
Seas of bright juice suffuse heaven.


The earth by the sky staid with, the daily close of their
        junction,
The heav'd challenge from the east that moment over my
        head,
The mocking taunt, See then whether you shall be master!


## 25

Dazzling and tremendous how quick the sun-rise would
        kill me,
If I could not now and always send sun-rise out of me.


We also ascend dazzling and tremendous as the sun,
We found our own O my soul in the calm and cool of the
        day-break.


My voice goes after what my eyes cannot reach,
With the twirl of my tongue I encompass worlds and
        volumes of worlds.


Speech is the twin of my vision, it is unequal to measure
        itself,
It provokes me forever, it says sarcastically,
*Walt you contain enough, why don't you let it out then?*

Come now I will not be tantalized, you conceive too much of articulation,
Do you not know O speech how the buds beneath you are folded?
Waiting in gloom, protected by frost,
The dirt receding before my prophetical screams,
I underlying causes to balance them at last,
My knowledge my live parts, it keeping tally with the meaning of all things,
Happiness, (which whoever hears me let him or her set out in search of this day.)


My final merit I refuse you, I refuse putting from me what I really am,
Encompass worlds, but never try to encompass me,
I crowd your sleekest and best by simply looking toward you.


Writing and talk do not prove me,
I carry the plenum of proof and every thing else in my face,
With the hush of my lips I wholly confound the skeptic.


26

Now I will do nothing but listen,
To accrue what I hear into this song, to let sounds contribute toward it.

I hear bravuras of birds, bustle of growing wheat, gossip of
        flames, clack of sticks cooking my meals,
I hear the sound I love, the sound of the human voice,
I hear all sounds running together, combined, fused or
        following,
Sounds of the city and sounds out of the city, sounds of the
        day and night,
Talkative young ones to those that like them, the loud laugh
        of work-people at their meals,
The angry base of disjointed friendship, the faint tones of
        the sick,
The judge with hands tight to the desk, his pallid lips pro-
        nouncing a death-sentence,
The heave'e'yo of stevedores unlading ships by the wharves,
        the refrain of the anchor-lifters,
The ring of alarm-bells, the cry of fire, the whirr of swift-
        streaking engines and hose-carts with premonitory
        tinkles and color'd lights,
The steam-whistle, the solid roll of the train of approach-
        ing cars,
The slow march play'd at the head of the association march-
        ing two and two,
(They go to guard some corpse, the flag-tops are draped
        with black muslin.)

I hear the violoncello, ('tis the young man's heart's com-
        plaint,)
I hear the key'd cornet, it glides quickly in through my
        ears,
It shakes mad-sweet pangs through my belly and breast.

I hear the chorus, it is a grand opera,
Ah this indeed is music—this suits me.

A tenor large and fresh as the creation fills me,
The orbic flex of his mouth is pouring and filling me full.

I hear the train'd soprano (what work with hers is this?)
The orchestra whirls me wider than Uranus flies,
It wrenches such ardors from me I did not know I possess'd
them,
It sails me, I dab with bare feet, they are lick'd by the
indolent waves,
I am cut by bitter and angry hail, I lose my breath,
Steep'd amid honey'd morphine, my windpipe throttled in
fakes of death,
At length let up again to feel the puzzle of puzzles,
And that we call Being.


## 27

To be in any form, what is that?
(Round and round we go, all of us, and ever come back
thither,)
If nothing lay more develop'd the quahaug in its callous
shell were enough.

Mine is no callous shell,
I have instant conductors all over me whether I pass or
stop,
They seize every object and lead it harmlessly through me.

I merely stir, press, feel with my fingers, and am happy,
To touch my person to some one else's is about as much as
       I can stand.

## 28

Is this then a touch? quivering me to a new identity,
Flames and ether making a rush for my veins,
Treacherous tip of me reaching and crowding to help them,
My flesh and blood playing out lightning to strike what is
       hardly different from myself,
On all sides prurient provokers stiffening my limbs,
Straining the udder of my heart for its withheld drip,
Behaving licentious toward me, taking no denial,
Depriving me of my best as for a purpose,
Unbuttoning my clothes, holding me by the bare waist,
Deluding my confusion with the calm of the sunlight and
       pasture-fields,
Immodestly sliding the fellow-senses away,
They bribed to swap off with touch and go and graze at the
       edges of me,
No consideration, no regard for my draining strength or
       my anger,
Fetching the rest of the herd around to enjoy them a while,
Then all uniting to stand on a headland and worry me.

The sentries desert every other part of me,
They have left me helpless to a red marauder,
They all come to the headland to witness and assist against
       me.

I am given up by traitors,
I talk wildly, I have lost my wits, I and nobody else am the
      greatest traitor,
I went myself first to the headland, my own hands carried
      me there.

You villain touch! what are you doing? my breath is tight
      in its throat,
Unclench your floodgates, you are too much for me.


## 29

Blind loving wrestling touch, sheath'd hooded sharp-tooth'd
      touch!
Did it make you ache so, leaving me?

Parting track'd by arriving, perpetual payment of perpetual
      loan,
Rich showering rain, and recompense richer afterward.

Sprouts take and accumulate, stand by the curb prolific and
      vital,
Landscapes projected masculine, full-sized and golden.


## 30

All truths wait in all things,
They neither hasten their own delivery nor resist it,
They do not need the obstetric forceps of the surgeon,

The insignificant is as big to me as any,
(What is less or more than a touch?)

Logic and sermons never convince,
The damp of the night drives deeper into my soul.

(Only what proves itself to every man and woman is so,
Only what nobody denies is so.)

A minute and a drop of me settle my brain,
I believe the soggy clods shall become lovers and lamps,
And a compend of compends is the meat of a man or
      woman,
And a summit and flower there is the feeling they have for
      each other,
And they are to branch boundlessly out of that lesson until
      it becomes omnific,
And until one and all shall delight us, and we them.


31

I believe a leaf of grass is no less than the journey-work of
      the stars,
And the pismire is equally perfect, and a grain of sand, and
      the egg of the wren,
And the tree-toad is a chef-d'œuvre for the highest,
And the running blackberry would adorn the parlors of
      heaven,
And the narrowest hinge in my hand puts to scorn all
      machinery,

And the cow crunching with depress'd head surpasses any
       statue,
And a mouse is miracle enough to stagger sextillions of
       infidels.


I find I incorporate gneiss, coal, long-threaded moss, fruits,
       grains, esculent roots,
And am stucco'd with quadrupeds and birds all over,
And have distanced what is behind me for good reasons,
But call any thing back again when I desire it.


In vain the speeding or shyness,
In vain the plutonic rocks send their old heat against my
       approach,
In vain the mastodon retreats beneath its own powder'd
       bones,
In vain objects stand leagues off and assume manifold
       shapes,
In vain the ocean settling in hollows and the great monsters
       lying low,
In vain the buzzard houses herself with the sky,
In vain the snake slides through the creepers and logs,
In vain the elk takes to the inner passes of the woods,
In vain the razor-bill'd auk sails far north to Labrador,
I follow quickly, I ascend to the nest in the fissure of the
       cliff.

## 32

I think I could turn and live with animals, they are so placid
    and self-contain'd,
I stand and look at them long and long.


They do not sweat and whine about their condition,
They do not lie awake in the dark and weep for their sins,
They do not make me sick discussing their duty to God,
Not one is dissatisfied, not one is demented with the mania
    of owning things,
Not one kneels to another, nor to his kind that lived thou-
    sands of years ago,
Not one is respectable or unhappy over the whole earth.


So they show their relations to me and I accept them,
They bring me tokens of myself, they evince them plainly
    in their possession.


I wonder where they get those tokens,
Did I pass that way huge times ago and negligently drop
    them?


Myself moving forward then and now and forever,
Gathering and showing more always and with velocity,
Infinite and omnigenous, and the like of these among them,
Not too exclusive toward the reachers of my remembrancers,
Picking out here one that I love, and now go with him on
    brotherly terms.

A gigantic beauty of a stallion, fresh and responsive to my
  caresses,
Head high in the forehead, wide between the ears,
Limbs glossy and supple, tail dusting the ground,
Eyes full of sparkling wickedness, ears finely cut, flexibly
  moving.

His nostrils dilate as my heels embrace him,
His well-built limbs tremble with pleasure as we race
  around and return.

I but use you a minute, then I resign you, stallion,
Why do I need your paces when I myself out-gallop them?
Even as I stand or sit passing faster than you.


### 33

Space and Time! now I see it is true, what I guess'd at,
What I guess'd when I loaf'd on the grass,
What I guess'd while I lay alone in my bed,
And again as I walk'd the beach under the paling stars of
  the morning.

My ties and ballasts leave me, my elbows rest in sea-gaps,
I skirt sierras, my palms cover continents,
I am afoot with my vision.

By the city's quadrangular houses—in log huts, camping
     with lumbermen,
Along the ruts of the turnpike, along the dry gulch and
     rivulet bed,
Weeding my onion-patch or hoeing rows of carrots and
     parsnips, crossing savannas, trailing in forests,
Prospecting, gold-digging, girdling the trees of a new pur-
     chase,
Scorch'd ankle-deep by the hot sand, hauling my boat down
     the shallow river,
When the panther walks to and fro on a limb overhead,
     where the buck turns furiously at the hunter,
Where the rattlesnake suns his flabby length on a rock,
     where the otter is feeding on fish,
Where the alligator in his tough pimples sleeps by the
     bayou,
Where the black bear is searching for roots or honey, where
     the beaver pats the mud with his paddle-shaped tail;
Over the growing sugar, over the yellow-flower'd cotton
     plant, over the rice in its low moist field,
Over the sharp-peak'd farm house, with its scallop'd scum
     and slender shoots from the gutters,
Over the western persimmon, over the long-leav'd corn,
     over the delicate blue-flower flax,
Over the white and brown buckwheat, a hummer and buz-
     zer there with the rest,
Over the dusky green of the rye as it ripples and shades in
     the breeze;
Scaling mountains, pulling myself cautiously up, holding
     on by low scragged limbs,

Walking the path worn in the grass and beat through the
leaves of the brush,

Where the quail is whistling betwixt the woods and the
wheat-lot,

Where the bat flies in the Seventh-month eve, where the
great goldbug drops through the dark,

Where the brook puts out of the roots of the old tree and
flows to the meadow,

Where cattle stand and shake away flies with the tremulous
shuddering of their hides,

Where the cheese-cloth hangs in the kitchen, where andirons
straddle the hearth-slab, where cobwebs fall in
festoons from the rafters;

Where trip-hammers crash, where the press is whirling its
cylinders,

Wherever the human heart beats with terrible throes under
its ribs,

Where the pear-shaped balloon is floating aloft, (floating in
it myself and looking composedly down,)

Where the life-car is drawn on the slip-noose, where the
heat hatches pale-green eggs in the dented sand,

Where the she-whale swims with her calf and never for-
sakes it,

Where the steam-ship trails hind-ways its long pennant of
smoke,

Where the fin of the shark cuts like a black chip out of the
water,

Where the half-burn'd brig is riding on unknown currents,

Where shells grow to her slimy deck, where the dead are
corrupting below;

Where the dense-starr'd flag is borne at the head of the
    regiments,
Approaching Manhattan up by the long-stretching island,
Under Niagara, the cataract falling like a veil over my
    countenance,
Upon a door-step, upon the horse-block of hard wood out-
    side,
Upon the race-course, or enjoying picnics or jigs or a good
    game of base-ball,
At he-festivals, with blackguard gibes, ironical license, bull-
    dances, drinking, laughter,
At the cider-mill tasting the sweets of the brown mash,
    sucking the juice through a straw,
At apple-peelings wanting kisses for all the red fruit I find,
At musters, beach-parties, friendly bees, huskings, house-
    raisings;
Where the mocking-bird sounds his delicious gurgles,
    cackles, screams, weeps,
Where the hay-rick stands in the barn-yard, where the dry-
    stalks are scatter'd, where the brood-cow waits in
    the hovel,
Where the bull advances to do his masculine work, where
    the stud to the mare, where the cock is treading the
    hen,
Where the heifers browse, where geese nip their food with
    short jerks,
Where sun-down shadows lengthen over the limitless and
    lonesome prairie,
Where herds of buffalo make a crawling spread of the
    square miles far and near,

Where the humming-bird shimmers, where the neck of the
long-lived swan is curving and winding,
Where the laughing-gull scoots by the shore, where she
laughs her near-human laugh,
Where bee-hives range on a gray bench in the garden half
hid by the high weeds,
Where band-neck'd partridges roost in a ring on the ground
with their heads out,
Where burial coaches enter the arch'd gates of a cemetery,
Where winter wolves bark amid wastes of snow and icicled
trees,
Where the yellow-crown'd heron comes to the edge of the
marsh at night and feeds upon small crabs,
Where the splash of swimmers and divers cools the warm
noon,
Where the katy-did works her chromatic reed on the walnut-
tree over the well,
Through patches of citrons and cucumbers with silver-wired
leaves,
Through the salt-lick or orange glade, or under conical firs,
Through the gymnasium, through the curtain'd saloon,
through the office or public hall;
Pleas'd with the native and pleas'd with the foreign, pleas'd
with the new and old,
Pleas'd with the homely woman as well as the handsome,
Pleas'd with the quakeress as she puts off her bonnet and
talks melodiously,
Pleas'd with the tune of the choir of the whitewash'd church,
Pleas'd with the earnest words of the sweating Methodist
preacher, impress'd seriously at the camp-meeting;

74

Looking in at the shop-windows of Broadway the whole forenoon, flatting the flesh of my nose on the thick plate glass,
Wandering the same afternoon with my face turn'd up to the clouds, or down a lane or along the beach,
My right and left arms round the sides of two friends, and I in the middle;
Coming home with the silent and dark-cheek'd bush-boy, (behind me he rides at the drape of the day,)
Far from the settlements studying the print of animals' feet, or the moccasin print,
By the cot in the hospital reaching lemonade to a feverish patient,
Nigh the coffin'd corpse when all is still, examining with a candle;
Voyaging to every port to dicker and adventure,
Hurrying with the modern crowd as eager and fickle as any,
Hot toward one I hate, ready in my madness to knife him,
Solitary at midnight in my back yard, my thoughts gone from me a long while,
Walking the old hills of Judæa with the beautiful gentle God by my side,
Speeding through space, speeding through heaven and the stars,
Speeding amid the seven satellites and the broad ring, and the diameter of eighty thousand miles,
Speeding with tail'd meteors, throwing fire-balls like the rest,
Carrying the crescent child that carries its own full mother in its belly,

75

Storming, enjoying, planning, loving, cautioning,
Backing and filling, appearing and disappearing,
I tread day and night such roads.

I visit the orchards of spheres and look at the product,
And look at quintillions ripen'd and look at quintillions
      green.

I fly those flights of a fluid and swallowing soul,
My course runs below the soundings of plummets.

I help myself to material and immaterial,
No guard can shut me off, no law prevent me.

I anchor my ship for a little while only,
My messengers continually cruise away or bring their re-
      turns to me.

I go hunting polar furs and the seal, leaping chasms with a
      pike-pointed staff, clinging to topples of brittle and
      blue.

I ascend to the foretruck,
I take my place late at night in the crow's-nest,
We sail the arctic sea, it is plenty light enough,
Through the clear atmosphere I stretch around on the won-
      derful beauty,

The enormous masses of ice pass me and I pass them, the
　　scenery is plain in all directions,
The white-topt mountains show in the distance, I fling out
　　my fancies toward them,
We are approaching some great battle-field in which we are
　　soon to be engaged,
We pass the colossal outposts of the encampment, we pass
　　with still feet and caution,
Or we are entering by the suburbs some vast and ruin'd city,
The blocks and fallen architecture more than all the living
　　cities of the globe.

I am a free companion, I bivouac by invading watchfires,
I turn the bridegroom out of bed and stay with the bride
　　myself,
I tighten her all night to my thighs and lips.

My voice is the wife's voice, the screech by the rail of the
　　stairs,
They fetch my man's body up dripping and drown'd.

I understand the large hearts of heroes,
The courage of present times and all times,
How the skipper saw the crowded and rudderless wreck of
　　the steam-ship, and Death chasing it up and down
　　the storm,
How he knuckled tight and gave not back an inch, and was
　　faithful of days and faithful of nights,
And chalk'd in large letters on a board, *Be of good cheer,
we will not desert you;*

How he follow'd with them and tack'd with them three
days and would not give it up,
How he saved the drifting company at last,
How the lank loose-gown'd women look'd when boated
from the side of their prepared graves,
How the silent old-faced infants and the lifted sick, and
the sharp-lipp'd unshaved men;
All this I swallow, it tastes good, I like it well, it becomes
mine,
I am the man, I suffer'd, I was there.

The disdain and calmness of martyrs,
The mother of old, condemn'd for a witch, burnt with dry
wood, her children gazing on,
The hounded slave that flags in the race, leans by the fence,
blowing, cover'd with sweat,
The twinges that sting like needles his legs and neck, the
murderous buckshot and the bullets,
All these I feel or am.

I am the hounded slave, I wince at the bite of the dogs,
Hell and despair are upon me, crack and again crack the
marksmen,
I clutch the rails of the fence, my gore dribs, thinn'd with
the ooze of my skin,
I fall on the weeds and stones,
The riders spur their unwilling horses, haul close,
Taunt my dizzy ears and beat me violently over the head
with whip-stocks.

Agonies are one of my changes of garments,
I do not ask the wounded person how he feels, I myself
        become the wounded person,
My hurts turn livid upon me as I lean on a cane and observe.

I am the mash'd fireman with breast-bone broken,
Tumbling walls buried me in their debris,
Heat and smoke I inspired, I heard the yelling shouts of my
        comrades,
I heard the distant click of their picks and shovels,
They have clear'd the beams away, they tenderly lift me
        forth.

I lie in the night air in my red shirt, the pervading hush is
        for my sake,
Painless after all I lie exhausted but not so unhappy,
White and beautiful are the faces around me, the heads are
        bared of their fire-caps,
The kneeling crowd fades with the light of the torches.

Distant and dead resuscitate,
They show as the dial or move as the hands of me, I am the
        clock myself.

I am an old artillerist, I tell of my fort's bombardment,
I am there again.

Again the long roll of the drummers,
Again the attacking cannon, mortars,
Again to my listening ears the cannon responsive.

79

I take part, I see and hear the whole,
The cries, curses, roar, the plaudits for well-aim'd shots,
The ambulanza slowly passing trailing its red drip,
Workmen searching after damages, making indispensable
       repairs,
The fall of grenades through the rent roof, the fan-shaped
       explosion,
The whizz of limbs, heads, stone, wood, iron, high in the
       air.


Again gurgles the mouth of my dying general, he furiously
       waves with his hand,
He gasps through the clot *Mind not me—mind—the en-*
       *trenchments.*


### 34

Now I tell what I knew in Texas in my early youth,
(I tell not the fall of Alamo,
Not one escaped to tell the fall of Alamo,
The hundred and fifty are dumb yet at Alamo,)
'Tis the tale of the murder in cold blood of four hundred
       and twelve young men.


Retreating they had form'd in a hollow square with their
       baggage for breastworks,
Nine hundred lives out of the surrounding enemy's, nine
       times their number, was the price they took in ad-
       vance,

Their colonel was wounded and their ammunition gone,
They treated for an honorable capitulation, receiv'd writing
and seal, gave up their arms and march'd back
prisoners of war.


They were the glory of the race of rangers,
Matchless with horse, rifle, song, supper, courtship,
Large, turbulent, generous, handsome, proud, and affec-
tionate,
Bearded, sunburnt, drest in the free costume of hunters,
Not a single one over thirty years of age.


The second First-day morning they were brought out in
squads and massacred, it was beautiful early sum-
mer,
The work commenced about five o'clock and was over by
eight.


None obey'd the command to kneel,
Some made a mad and helpless rush, some stood stark and
straight,
A few fell at once, shot in the temple or heart, the living
and dead lay together,
The maim'd and mangled dug in the dirt, the new-comers
saw them there,
Some half-kill'd attempted to crawl away,
These were despatch'd with bayonets or batter'd with the
blunts of muskets,

A youth not seventeen years old seiz'd his assassin till two
more came to release him,
The three were all torn and cover'd with the boy's blood.

At eleven o'clock began the burning of the bodies;
That is the tale of the murder of the four hundred and
twelve young men.


## 35

Would you hear of an old-time sea-fight?
Would you learn who won by the light of the moon and
stars?
List to the yarn, as my grandmother's father the sailor told
it to me.

Our foe was no skulk in his ship I tell you, (said he,)
His was the surly English pluck, and there is no tougher or
truer, and never was, and never will be;
Along the lower'd eve he came horribly raking us.

We closed with him, the yards entangled, the cannon
touch'd,
My captain lash'd fast with his own hands.

We had receiv'd some eighteen pound shots under the
water,
On our lower-gun-deck two large pieces had burst at the
first fire, killing all around and blowing up over-
head.

Fighting at sun-down, fighting at dark,
Ten o'clock at night, the full moon well up, our leaks on
      the gain, and five feet of water reported,
The master-at-arms loosing the prisoners confined in the
      after-hold to give them a chance for themselves.


The transit to and from the magazine is now stopt by the
      sentinels,
They see so many strange faces they do not know whom to
      trust.


Our frigate takes fire,
The other asks if we demand quarter?
If our colors are struck and the fighting done?


Now I laugh content, for I hear the voice of my little
      captain,
*We have not struck,* he composedly cries, *we have just
      begun our part of the fighting.*


Only three guns are in use,
One is directed by the captain himself against the enemy's
      mainmast,
Two well serv'd with grape and canister silence his musketry
      and clear his decks.


The tops alone second the fire of this little battery, espe-
      cially the main-top,
They hold out bravely during the whole of the action.

Not a moment's cease,
The leaks gain fast on the pumps, the fire eats toward the
      powder-magazine.


One of the pumps has been shot away, it is generally
      thought we are sinking.


Serene stands the little captain,
He is not hurried, his voice is neither high nor low,
His eyes give more light to us than our battle-lanterns.


Toward twelve there in the beams of the moon they sur-
      render to us.


## 36

Stretch'd and still lies the midnight,
Two great hulls motionless on the breast of the darkness,
Our vessel riddled and slowly sinking, preparations to pass
      to the one we have conquer'd,
The captain on the quarter-deck coldly giving his orders
      through a countenance white as a sheet,
Near by the corpse of the child that serv'd in the cabin,
The dead face of an old salt with long white hair and care-
      fully curl'd whiskers,
The flames spite of all that can be done flickering aloft and
      ' below,
The husky voices of the two or three officers yet fit for duty,

Formless stacks of bodies and bodies by themselves, dabs of
 flesh upon the masts and spars,
Cut of cordage, dangle of rigging, slight shock of the
 soothe of waves,
Black and impassive guns, litter of powder-parcels, strong
 scent,
A few large stars overhead, silent and mournful shining,
Delicate sniffs of sea-breeze, smells of sedgy grass and fields
 by the shore, death-messages given in charge to
 survivors,
The hiss of the surgeon's knife, the gnawing teeth of his
 saw,
Wheeze, cluck, swash of falling blood, short wild scream,
 and long, dull, tapering groan,
These so, these irretrievable.


## 37

You laggards there on guard! look to your arms!
In at the conquer'd doors they crowd! I am possess'd!
Embody all presences outlaw'd or suffering,
See myself in prison shaped like another man,
And feel the dull unintermitted pain.

For me the keepers of convicts shoulder their carbines and
 keep watch,
It is I let out in the morning and barr'd at night.

Not a mutineer walks handcuff'd to jail but I am handcuff'd
 to him and walk by his side,

(I am less the jolly one there, and more the silent one with
    sweat on my twitching lips.)


Not a youngster is taken for larceny but I go up too, and am
    tried and sentenced.


Not a cholera patient lies at the last gasp but I also lie at the
    last gasp,
My face is ash-color'd, my sinews gnarl, away from me peo-
    ple retreat.


Askers embody themselves in me and I am embodied in
    them,
I project my hat, sit shame-faced, and beg.


## 38

Enough! enough! enough!
Somehow I have been stunn'd. Stand back!
Give me a little time beyond my cuff'd head, slumbers,
    dreams, gaping,
I discover myself on the verge of a usual mistake.


That I could forget the mockers and insults!
That I could forget the trickling tears and the blows of
    the bludgeons and hammers!
That I could look with a separate look on my own crucifixion
    and bloody crowning.

I remember now,
I resume the overstaid fraction,
The grave of rock multiplies what has been confided to it,
        or to any graves,
Corpses rise, gashes heal, fastenings roll from me.

I troop forth replenish'd with supreme power, one of an
        average unending procession,
Inland and sea-coast we go, and pass all boundary lines,
Our swift ordinances on their way over the whole earth,
The blossoms we wear in our hats the growth of thousands
        of years.

Eleves, I salute you! come forward!
Continue your annotations, continue your questionings.


### 39

The friendly and flowing savage, who is he?
Is he waiting for civilization, or past it and mastering it?

Is he some Southwesterner rais'd out-doors? is he Kanadian?
Is he from the Mississippi country? Iowa, Oregon, Cali-
        fornia?
The mountains? prairie-life, bush-life? or sailor from the
        sea?

Wherever he goes men and women accept and desire him,
They desire he should like them, touch them, speak to them,
        stay with them.

Behavior lawless as snow-flakes, words simple as grass, un-
      comb'd head, laughter, and naivetè,
Slow-stepping feet, common features, common modes and
      emanations,
They descend in new forms from the tips of his fingers,
They are wafted with the odor of his body or breath, they fly
      out of the glance of his eyes.


40

Flaunt of the sunshine I need not your bask—lie over!
You light surfaces only, I force surfaces and depths also.

Earth! you seem to look for something at my hands,
Say, old top-knot, what do you want?

Man or woman, I might tell how I like you, but cannot,
And might tell what it is in me and what it is in you, but
      cannot,
And might tell that pining I have, that pulse of my nights
      and days.

Behold, I do not give lectures or a little charity,
When I give I give myself.

You there, impotent, loose in the knees,
Open your scarf'd chops till I blow grit within you,
Spread your palms and lift the flaps of your pockets,

I am not to be denied, I compel, I have stores plenty and to
    spare,
And any thing I have I bestow.

I do not ask who you are, that is not important to me,
You can do nothing and be nothing but what I will infold
    you.

To cotton-field drudge or cleaner of privies I lean,
On his right cheek I put the family kiss,
And in my soul I swear I never will deny him.

On women fit for conception I start bigger and nimbler
    babes,
(This day I am jetting the stuff of far more arrogant
    republics.)

To any one dying, thither I speed and twist the knob of the
    door,
Turn the bed-clothes toward the foot of the bed,
Let the physician and the priest go home.

I seize the descending man and raise him with resistless will,
O despairer, here is my neck,
By God, you shall not go down! hang your whole weight
    upon me.

I dilate you with tremendous breath, I buoy you up,
Every room of the house do I fill with an arm'd force,
Lovers of me, bafflers of graves.

Sleep—I and they keep guard all night,
Not doubt, not decease shall dare to lay finger upon you,
I have embraced you, and henceforth possess you to myself,
And when you rise in the morning you will find what I tell
      you is so.


41


I am he bringing help for the sick as they pant on their
      backs,
And for strong upright men I bring yet more needed help.

I heard what was said of the universe,
Heard it and heard it of several thousand years;
It is middling well as far as it goes—but is that all?

Magnifying and applying come I,
Outbidding at the start the old cautious hucksters,
Taking myself the exact dimensions of Jehovah,
Lithographing Kronos, Zeus his son, and Hercules his
      grandson,
Buying drafts of Osiris, Isis, Belus, Brahma, Buddha,
In my portfolio placing Manito loose, Allah on a leaf, the
      crucifix engraved,
With Odin and the hideous-faced Mexitli and every idol
      and image,
Taking them all for what they are worth and not a cent
      more,
Admitting they were alive and did the work of their days,

(They bore mites as for unfledg'd birds who have now to
      rise and fly and sing for themselves,)
Accepting the rough deific sketches to fill out better in my-
      self, bestowing them freely on each man and woman
      I see,
Discovering as much or more in a framer framing a house,
Putting higher claims for him there with his roll'd-up
      sleeves driving the mallet and chisel,
Not objecting to special revelations, considering a curl of
      smoke or a hair on the back of my hand just as
      curious as any revelation,
Lads ahold of fire-engines and hook-and-ladder ropes no
      less to me than the gods of the antique wars,
Minding their voices peal through the crash of destruction,
Their brawny limbs passing safe over charr'd laths, their
      white foreheads whole and unhurt out of the flames;
By the mechanic's wife with her babe at her nipple interced-
      ing for every person born,
Three scythes at harvest whizzing in a row from three lusty
      angels with shirts bagg'd out at their waists,
The snag-tooth'd hostler with red hair redeeming sins past
      and to come,
Selling all he possesses, traveling on foot to fee lawyers for
      his brother and sit by him while he is tried for
      forgery;
What was strewn in the amplest strewing the square rod
      about me, and not filling the square rod then,
The bull and the bug never worshipp'd half enough,
Dung and dirt more admirable than was dream'd,

The supernatural of no account, myself waiting my time to
    be one of the supremes,
The day getting ready for me when I shall do as much good
    as the best, and be as prodigious;
By my life-lumps! becoming already a creator,
Putting myself here and now to the ambush'd womb of the
    shadows.


42

A call in the midst of the crowd,
My own voice, orotund sweeping and final.


Come my children,
Come my boys and girls, my women, household and inti-
    mates,
Now the performer launches his nerve, he has pass'd his
    prelude on the reeds within.


Easily written loose-finger'd chords—I feel the thrum of
    your climax and close.


My head slues round on my neck,
Music rolls, but not from the organ,
Folks are around me, but they are no household of mine.


Ever the hard unsunk ground,
Ever the eaters and drinkers, ever the upward and down-
    ward sun, ever the air and the ceaseless tides,

Ever myself and my neighbors, refreshing, wicked, real,
Ever the old inexplicable query, ever that thorn'd thumb,
    that breath of itches and thirsts,
Ever the vexer's *hoot! hoot!* till we find where the sly one
    hides and bring him forth,
Ever love, ever the sobbing liquid of life,
Ever the bandage under the chin, ever the trestles of death.


Here and there with dimes on the eyes walking,
To feed the greed of the belly the brains liberally spooning,
Tickets buying, taking, selling, but in to the feast never
    once going,
Many sweating, ploughing, thrashing, and then the chaff
    for payment receiving,
A few idly owning, and they the wheat continually claiming.


This is the city and I am one of the citizens,
Whatever interests the rest interests me, politics, wars,
    markets, newspapers, schools,
The mayor and councils, banks, tariffs, steamships, fac-
    tories, stocks, stores, real estate and personal estate.


The little plentiful manikins skipping around in collars and
    tail'd coats,
I am aware who they are, (they are positively not worms or
    fleas,)
I acknowledge the duplicates of myself, the weakest and
    shallowest is deathless with me,
What I do and say the same waits for them,

Every thought that flounders in me the same flounders in
    them.

I know perfectly well my own egotism,
Know my omnivorous lines and must not write any less,
And would fetch you whoever you are flush with myself.

Not words of routine this song of mine,
But abruptly to question, to leap beyond yet nearer bring;
This printed and bound book—but the printer and the
    printing-office boy?
The well-taken photographs—but your wife or friend close
    and solid in your arms?
The black ship mail'd with iron, her mighty guns in her
    turrets—but the pluck of the captain and engineers?
In the houses the dishes and fare and furniture—but the
    host and hostess, and the look out of their eyes?
The sky up there—yet here or next door, or across the way?
The saints and sages in history—but you yourself?
Sermons, creeds, theology—but the fathomless human
    brain,
And what is reason? and what is love? and what is life?


43

I do not despise you priests, all time, the world over,
My faith is the greatest of faiths and the least of faiths,
Enclosing worship ancient and modern and all between
    ancient and modern,

Believing I shall come again upon the earth after five thousand years,

Waiting responses from oracles, honoring the gods, saluting the sun,

Making a fetich of the first rock or stump, powowing with sticks in the circle of obis,

Helping the llama or brahmin as he trims the lamps of the idols,

Dancing yet through the streets in a phallic procession, rapt and austere in the woods a gymnosophist,

Drinking mead from the skull-cup, to Shastas and Vedas admirant, minding the Koran,

Walking the teokallis, spotted with gore from the stone and knife, beating the serpent-skin drum,

Accepting the Gospels, accepting him that was crucified, knowing assuredly that he is divine,

To the mass kneeling or the puritan's prayer rising, or sitting patiently in a pew,

Ranting and frothing in my insane crisis, or waiting dead-like till my spirit arouses me,

Looking forth on pavement and land, or outside of pavement and land,

Belonging to the winders of the circuit of circuits.


One of that centripetal and centrifugal gang I turn and talk like a man leaving charges before a journey.


Down-hearted doubters dull and excluded,

Frivolous, sullen, moping, angry, affected, dishearten'd, atheistical,

I know every one of you, I know the sea of torment, doubt, despair and unbelief.

How the flukes splash!
How they contort rapid as lightning, with spasms and spouts of blood!

Be at peace bloody flukes of doubters and sullen mopers,
I take my place among you as much as among any,
The past is the push of you, me, all, precisely the same,
And what is yet untried and afterward is for you, me, all, precisely the same.

I do not know what is untried and afterward,
But I know it will in its turn prove sufficient, and cannot fail.

Each who passes is consider'd, each who stops is consider'd, not a single one can it fail.

It cannot fail the young man who died and was buried,
Nor the young woman who died and was put by his side,
Nor the little child that peep'd in at the door, and then drew back and was never seen again,
Nor the old man who has lived without purpose, and feels it with bitterness worse than gall,
Nor him in the poor house tubercled by rum and the bad disorder,
Nor the numberless slaughter'd and wreck'd, nor the brutish koboo call'd the ordure of humanity,

Nor the sacs merely floating with open mouths for food to
       slip in,
Nor any thing in the earth, or down in the oldest graves of
       the earth,
Nor any thing in the myriads of spheres, nor the myriads of
       myriads that inhabit them,
Nor the present, nor the least wisp that is known.


## 44

It is time to explain myself—let us stand up.

What is known I strip away,
I launch all men and women forward with me into the
       Unknown.

The clock indicates the moment—but what does eternity
       indicate?

We have thus far exhausted trillions of winters and sum-
       mers,
There are trillions ahead, and trillions ahead of them.

Births have brought us richness and variety,
And other births will bring us richness and variety.

I do not call one greater and one smaller,
That which fills its period and place is equal to any.

Were mankind murderous or jealous upon you, my brother,
       my sister?
I am sorry for you, they are not murderous or jealous upon
       me,
All has been gentle with me, I keep no account with lamenta-
       tion,
(What have I to do with lamentation?)

I am an acme of things accomplish'd, and I an encloser of
       things to be.

My feet strike an apex of the apices of the stairs,
On every step bunches of ages, and larger bunches between
       the steps,
All below duly travel'd, and still I mount and mount.

Rise after rise bow the phantoms behind me,
Afar down I see the huge first Nothing, I know I was even
       there,
I waited unseen and always, and slept through the lethargic
       mist,
And took my time, and took no hurt from the fetid carbon.

Long I was hugg'd close—long and long.

Immense have been the preparations for me,
Faithful and friendly the arms that have help'd me.

Cycles ferried my cradle, rowing and rowing like cheerful
       boatmen,

For room to me stars kept aside in their own rings,
They sent influences to look after what was to hold me.

Before I was born out of my mother generations guided me,
My embryo has never been torpid, nothing could overlay
  it.

For it the nebula cohered to an orb,
The long slow strata piled to rest it on,
Vast vegetables gave it sustenance,
Monstrous sauroids transported it in their mouths and de-
  posited it with care.

All forces have been steadily employ'd to complete and de-
  light me,
Now on this spot I stand with my robust soul.


### 45

O span of youth! ever-push'd elasticity!
O manhood, balanced, florid and full.

My lovers suffocate me,
Crowding my lips, thick in the pores of my skin,
Jostling me through streets and public halls, coming naked
  to me at night,
Crying by day *Ahoy!* from the rocks of the river, swinging
  and chirping over my head,
Calling my name from flower-beds, vines, tangled under-
  brush,

Lighting on every moment of my life,
Bussing my body with soft balsamic busses,
Noiselessly passing handfuls out of their hearts and giving
     them to be mine.


Old age superbly rising! O welcome, ineffable grace of dying
     days!


Every condition promulges not only itself, it promulges
     what grows after and out of itself,
And the dark hush promulges as much as any.


I open my scuttle at night and see the far-sprinkled systems,
And all I see multiplied as high as I can cipher edge but the
     rim of the farther systems.


Wider and wider they spread, expanding, always expand-
     ing,
Outward and outward and forever outward.


My sun has his sun and round him obediently wheels,
He joins with his partners a group of superior circuit,
And greater sets follow, making specks of the greatest in-
     side them.


There is no stoppage and never can be stoppage,
If I, you, and the worlds, and all beneath or upon their sur-
     faces, were this moment reduced back to a pallid
     float, it would not avail in the long run,

We should surely bring up again where we now stand,
And surely go as much farther, and then farther and farther.

A few quadrillions of eras, a few octillions of cubic leagues,
        do not hazard the span or make it impatient,
They are but parts, any thing is but a part.

See ever so far, there is limitless space outside of that,
Count ever so much, there is limitless time around that.

My rendezvous is appointed, it is certain,
The Lord will be there and wait till I come on perfect terms,
The great Camerado, the lover true for whom I pine will
        be there.


## 46

I know I have the best of time and space, and was never
        measured and never will be measured.

I tramp a perpetual journey, (come listen all!)
My signs are a rain-proof coat, good shoes, and a staff cut
        from the woods,
No friend of mine takes his ease in my chair,
I have no chair, no church, no philosophy,
I lead no man to a dinner-table, library, exchange,
But each man and each woman of you I lead upon a knoll,
My left hand hooking you round the waist,

My right hand pointing to landscapes of continents and the
    public road.

Not I, not any one else can travel that road for you,
You must travel it for yourself.

It is not far, it is within reach,
Perhaps you have been on it since you were born and did not
    know,
Perhaps it is everywhere on water and on land.

Shoulder your duds dear son, and I will mine, and let us
    hasten forth,
Wonderful cities and free nations we shall fetch as we go.

If you tire, give me both burdens, and rest the chuff of your
    hand on my hip,
And in due time you shall repay the same service to me,
For after we start we never lie by again.

This day before dawn I ascended a hill and look'd at the
    crowded heaven,
And I said to my spirit *When we become the enfolders of
    those orbs, and the pleasure and knowledge of every
    thing in them, shall we be fill'd and satisfied then?*
And my spirit said *No, we but level that lift to pass and
    continue beyond.*

You are also asking me questions and I hear you,
I answer that I cannot answer, you must find out for yourself.

Sit a while dear son,
Here are biscuits to eat and here is milk to drink,
But as soon as you sleep and renew yourself in sweet clothes,
      I kiss you with a good-by kiss and open the gate for
      your egress hence.

Long enough have you dream'd contemptible dreams,
Now I wash the gum from your eyes,
You must habit yourself to the dazzle of the light and of
      every moment of your life.

Long have you timidly waded holding a plank by the shore,
Now I will you to be a bold swimmer,
To jump off in the midst of the sea, rise again, nod to me,
      shout, and laughingly dash with your hair.

### 47

I am the teacher of athletes,
He that by me spreads a wider breast than my own proves the
      width of my own,
He most honors my style who learns under it to destroy the
      teacher.

The boy I love, the same becomes a man not through derived
      power, but in his own right,
Wicked rather than virtuous out of conformity or fear,
Fond of his sweetheart, relishing well his steak,
Unrequited love or a slight cutting him worse than sharp
      steel cuts,

First-rate to ride, to fight, to hit the bull's eye, to sail a skiff,
       to sing a song or play on the banjo,
Preferring scars and the beard and faces pitted with small-
       pox over all latherers,
And those well-tann'd to those that keep out of the sun.


I teach straying from me, yet who can stray from me?
I follow you whoever you are from the present hour,
My words itch at your ears till you understand them.


I do not say these things for a dollar or to fill up the time
       while I wait for a boat,
(It is you talking just as much as myself, I act as the tongue
       of you,
Tied in your mouth, in mine it begins to be loosen'd.)


I swear I will never again mention love or death inside a
       house,
And I swear I will never translate myself at all, only to him
       or her who privately stays with me in the open air.


If you would understand me go to the heights or water-
       shore,
The nearest gnat is an explanation, and a drop or motion of
       waves a key,
The maul, the oar, the hand-saw, second my words.


No shutter'd room or school can commune with me,
But roughs and little children better than they.

The young mechanic is closest to me, he knows me well,
The woodman that takes his axe and jug with him shall take
　　　me with him all day,
The farm-boy ploughing in the field feels good at the sound
　　　of my voice,
In vessels that sail my words sail, I go with fishermen and
　　　seamen and love them.


The soldier camp'd or upon the march is mine,
On the night ere the pending battle many seek me, and I do
　　　not fail them,
On that solemn night (it may be their last) those that know
　　　me seek me.


My face rubs to the hunter's face when he lies down alone in
　　　his blanket,
The driver thinking of me does not mind the jolt of his
　　　wagon,
The young mother and old mother comprehend me,
The girl and the wife rest the needle a moment and forget
　　　where they are,
They and all would resume what I have told them.


## 48

I have said that the soul is not more than the body,
And I have said that the body is not more than the soul,
And nothing, not God, is greater to one than one's self is,

And whoever walks a furlong without sympathy walks to
     his own funeral drest in his shroud,
And I or you pocketless of a dime may purchase the pick of
     the earth,
And to glance with an eye or show a bean in its pod con-
     founds the learning of all times,
And there is no trade or employment but the young man
     following it may become a hero,
And there is no object so soft but it makes a hub for the
     wheel'd universe,
And I say to any man or woman, Let your soul stand cool and
     composed before a million universes.

And I say to mankind, Be not curious about God,
For I who am curious about each am not curious about God,
(No array of terms can say how much I am at peace about
     God and about death.)

I hear and behold God in every object, yet understand God
     not in the least,
Nor do I understand who there can be more wonderful than
     myself.

Why should I wish to see God better than this day?
I see something of God each hour of the twenty-four, and
     each moment then,
In the faces of men and women I see God, and in my own
     face in the glass,
I find letters from God dropt in the street, and every one is
     sign'd by God's name,

And I leave them where they are, for I know that where-
     soe'er I go,
Others will punctually come for ever and ever.


### 49

And as to you Death, and you bitter hug of mortality, it is
     idle to try to alarm me.


To his work without flinching the accoucheur comes,
I see the elder-hand pressing receiving supporting,
I recline by the sills of the exquisite flexible doors,
And mark the outlet, and mark the relief and escape.


And as to you Corpse I think you are good manure, but that
     does not offend me,
I smell the white roses sweet-scented and growing,
I reach to the leafy lips, I reach to the polish'd breasts of
     melons.


And as to you Life I reckon you are the leavings of many
     deaths,
(No doubt I have died myself ten thousand times before.)


I hear you whispering there O stars of heaven,
O suns—O grass of graves—O perpetual transfers and pro-
     motions,
If you do not say any thing how can I say any thing?

Of the turbid pool that lies in the autumn forest,
Of the moon that descends the steeps of the soughing twi-
        light,
Toss, sparkles of day and dusk—toss on the black stems that
        decay in the muck,
Toss to the moaning gibberish of the dry limbs.


I ascend from the moon, I ascend from the night,
I perceive that the ghastly glimmer is noonday sunbeams
        reflected,
And debouch to the steady and central from the offspring
        great or small.


## 50

There is that in me—I do not know what it is—but I know
        it is in me.


Wrench'd and sweaty—calm and cool then my body be-
        comes,
I sleep—I sleep long.


I do not know it—it is without name—it is a word unsaid,
It is not in any dictionary, utterance, symbol.


Something it swings on more than the earth I swing on,
To it the creation is the friend whose embracing awakes me.

Perhaps I might tell more. Outlines! I plead for my brothers
      and sisters.

Do you see O my brothers and sisters?
It is not chaos or death—it is form, union, plan—it is eternal
      life—it is Happiness.


## 51

The past and present wilt—I have fill'd them, emptied them,
And proceed to fill my next fold of the future.

Listener up there! what have you to confide to me?
Look in my face while I snuff the sidle of evening,
(Talk honestly, no one else hears you, and I stay only a
      minute longer.)

Do I contradict myself?
Very well then I contradict myself,
(I am large, I contain multitudes.)

I concentrate toward them that are nigh, I wait on the door-
      slab.

Who has done his day's work? who will soonest be through
      with his supper?
Who wishes to walk with me?

Will you speak before I am gone? will you prove already
      too late?

## 52

The spotted hawk swoops by and accuses me, he complains
    of my gab and my loitering.

I too am not a bit tamed, I too am untranslatable,
I sound my barbaric yawp over the roofs of the world.

The last scud of day holds back for me,
It flings my likeness after the rest and true as any on the
    shadow'd wilds,
It coaxes me to the vapor and the dusk.

I depart as air, I shake my white locks at the runaway sun,
I effuse my flesh in eddies, and drift it in lacy jags.

I bequeath myself to the dirt to grow from the grass I love,
If you want me again look for me under your boot-soles.

You will hardly know who I am or what I mean,
But I shall be good health to you nevertheless,
And filter and fibre your blood.

Failing to fetch me at first keep encouraged,
Missing me one place search another,
I stop somewhere waiting for you.

# Children of Adam

## TO THE GARDEN THE WORLD

To the garden the world anew ascending,
Potent mates, daughters, sons, preluding,
The love, the life of their bodies, meaning and being,
Curious here behold my resurrection after slumber,
The revolving cycles in their wide sweep having brought me
   again,
Amorous, mature, all beautiful to me, all wondrous,
My limbs and the quivering fire that ever plays through
   them, for reasons, most wondrous,
Existing I peer and penetrate still,
Content with the present, content with the past,
By my side or back of me Eve following,
Or in front, and I following her just the same.

## ONE HOUR TO MADNESS AND JOY

One hour to madness and joy! O furious! O confine me not!
(What is this that frees me so in storms?
What do my shouts amid lightnings and raging winds
   mean?)

O to drink the mystic deliria deeper than any other man!
O savage and tender achings! (I bequeath them to you my
     children,
I tell them to you, for reasons, O bridegroom and bride.)


O to be yielded to you whoever you are, and you to be
     yielded to me in defiance of the world!
O to return to Paradise! O bashful and feminine!
O to draw you to me, to plant on you for the first time the
     lips of a determin'd man.


O the puzzle, the thrice-tied knot, the deep and dark pool, all
     untied and illumin'd!
O to speed where there is space enough and air enough at
     last!
To be absolv'd from previous ties and conventions, I from
     mine and you from yours!
To find a new unthought-of nonchalance with the best of
     Nature!
To have the gag remov'd from one's mouth!
To have the feeling to-day or any day I am sufficient as I am.


O something unprov'd! something in a trance!
To escape utterly from others' anchors and holds!
To drive free! to love free! to dash reckless and dangerous!
To court destruction with taunts, with invitations!
To ascend, to leap to the heavens of the love indicated to
     me!
To rise thither with my inebriate soul!

To be lost if it must be so!
To feed the remainder of life with one hour of fulness and
        freedom!
With one brief hour of madness and joy.


## OUT OF THE ROLLING OCEAN THE CROWD

Out of the rolling ocean the crowd came a drop gently to
        me,
Whispering *I love you, before long I die,*
*I have travel'd a long way merely to look on you to touch*
        *you,*
*For I could not die till I once look'd on you,*
*For I fear'd I might afterward lose you.*


Now we have met, we have look'd, we are safe,
Return in peace to the ocean my love,
I too am part of that ocean my love, we are not so much
        separated,
Behold the great rondure, the cohesion of all, how perfect!
But as for me, for you, the irresistible sea is to separate us,
As for an hour carrying us diverse, yet cannot carry us
        diverse forever;
Be not impatient—a little space—know you I salute the air,
        the ocean and the land,
Every day at sundown for your dear sake my love.

# AGES AND AGES RETURNING AT INTERVALS

Ages and ages returning at intervals,
Undestroy'd, wandering immortal,
Lusty, phallic, with the potent original loins, perfectly sweet,
I, chanter of Adamic songs,
Through the new garden the West, the great cities calling,
Deliriate, thus prelude what is generated, offering these,
        offering myself,
Bathing myself, bathing my songs in Sex,
Offspring of my loins.

# WE TWO, HOW LONG WE WERE FOOL'D

We two, how long we were fool'd,
Now transmuted, we swiftly escape as Nature escapes,
We are Nature, long have we been absent, but now we
        return,
We become plants, trunks, foliage, roots, bark,
We are bedded in the ground, we are rocks,
We are oaks, we grow in the openings side by side,
We browse, we are two among the wild herds spontaneous
        as any,
We are two fishes swimming in the sea together,
We are what locust blossoms are, we drop scent around lanes
        mornings and evenings,
We are also the coarse smut of beasts, vegetables, minerals,
We are two predatory hawks, we soar above and look down,

We are two resplendent suns, we it is who balance ourselves
        orbic and stellar, we are as two comets,
We prowl fang'd and four-footed in the woods, we spring
        on prey,
We are two clouds forenoons and afternoons driving over-
        head,
We are seas mingling, we are two of those cheerful waves
        rolling over each other and interwetting each other,
We are what the atmosphere is, transparent, receptive, per-
        vious, impervious,
We are snow, rain, cold, darkness, we are each product and
        influence of the globe,
We have circled and circled till we have arrived home again,
        we two,
We have voided all but freedom and all but our own joy.


## O HYMEN! O HYMENEE!

O hymen! O hymenee! why do you tantalize me thus?
O why sting me for a swift moment only?
Why can you not continue? O why do you now cease?
Is it because if you continued beyond the swift moment you
        would soon certainly kill me?


## ONCE I PASS'D THROUGH A POPULOUS CITY

Once I pass'd through a populous city imprinting my brain
        for future use with its shows, architecture, customs,
        traditions,

Yet now of all that city I remember only a woman I casually met there who detain'd me for love of me,

Day by day and night by night we were together—all else has long been forgotten by me,

I remember I say only that woman who passionately clung to me,

Again we wander, we love, we separate again,

Again she holds me by the hand, I must not go,

I see her close beside me with silent lips sad and tremulous.

## I HEARD YOU SOLEMN-SWEET PIPES OF THE ORGAN

I heard you solemn-sweet pipes of the organ as last Sunday morn I pass'd the church,

Winds of autumn, as I walk'd the woods at dusk I heard your long-stretch'd sighs up above so mournful,

I heard the perfect Italian tenor singing at the opera, I heard the soprano in the midst of the quartet singing;

Heart of my love! you too I heard murmuring low through one of the wrists around my head,

Heard the pulse of you when all was still ringing little bells last night under my ear.

# FACING WEST FROM CALIFORNIA'S SHORES

Facing west from California's shores,
Inquiring, tireless, seeking what is yet unfound,
I, a child, very old, over waves, towards the house of maternity, the land of migrations, look afar,
Look off the shores of my Western sea, the circle almost circled;
For starting westward from Hindustan, from the vales of Kashmere,
From Asia, from the north, from the God, the sage, and the hero,
From the south, from the flowery peninsulas and the spice islands,
Long having wander'd since, round the earth having wander'd,
Now I face home again, very pleas'd and joyous,
(But where is what I started for so long ago?
And why is it yet unfound?)


# AS ADAM EARLY IN THE MORNING

As Adam early in the morning,
Walking forth from the bower refresh'd with sleep,
Behold me where I pass, hear my voice, approach,
Touch me, touch the palm of your hand to my body as I pass,
Be not afraid of my body.

# Calamus

## IN PATHS UNTRODDEN

In paths untrodden,
In the growth by margins of pond-waters,
Escaped from the life that exhibits itself,
From all the standards hitherto publish'd, from the pleas-
       ures, profits, conformities,
Which too long I was offering to feed my soul,
Clear to me now standards not yet publish'd, clear to me
       that my soul,
That the soul of the man I speak for rejoices in comrades,
Here by myself away from the clank of the world,
Tallying and talk'd to here by tongues aromatic,
No longer abash'd, (for in this secluded spot I can respond
       as I would not dare elsewhere,)
Strong upon me the life that does not exhibit itself, yet con-
       tains all the rest,
Resolv'd to sing no songs to-day but those of manly attach-
       ment,
Projecting them along that substantial life,
Bequeathing hence types of athletic love,

Afternoon this delicious Ninth-month in my forty-first year,
I proceed for all who are or have been young men,
To tell the secret of my nights and days,
To celebrate the need of comrades.


## SCENTED HERBAGE OF MY BREAST

Scented herbage of my breast,
Leaves from you I glean, I write, to be perused best after-
      wards,
Tomb-leaves, body-leaves growing up above me above
      death,
Perennial roots, tall leaves, O the winter shall not freeze you
      delicate leaves,
Every year shall you bloom again, out from where you re-
      tired you shall emerge again;
O I do not know whether many passing by will discover you
      or inhale your faint odor, but I believe a few will;
O slender leaves! O blossoms of my blood! I permit you to
      tell in your own way of the heart that is under you,
O I do not know what you mean there underneath your-
      selves, you are not happiness,
You are often more bitter than I can bear, you burn and
      sting me,
Yet you are beautiful to me you faint tinged roots, you make
      me think of death,
Death is beautiful from you, (what indeed is finally beau-
      tiful except death and love?)

O I think it is not for life I am chanting here my chant of
lovers, I think it must be for death,
For how calm, how solemn it grows to ascend to the atmos-
phere of lovers,
Death or life I am then indifferent, my soul declines to pre-
fer,
(I am not sure but the high soul of lovers welcomes death
most,)
Indeed O death, I think now these leaves mean precisely
the same as you mean,
Grow up taller sweet leaves that I may see! grow up out of
my breast!
Spring away from the conceal'd heart there!
Do not fold yourself so in your pink-tinged roots timid
leaves!
Do not remain down there so ashamed, herbage of my
breast!
Come I am determin'd to unbare this broad breast of mine,
I have long enough stifled and choked;
Emblematic and capricious blades I leave you, now you serve
me not,
I will say what I have to say by itself,
I will sound myself and comrades only, I will never again
utter a call only their call,
I will raise with it immortal reverberations through the
States,
I will give an example to lovers to take permanent shape and
will through the States,
Through me shall the words be said to make death exhila-
rating,

Give me your tone therefore O death, that I may accord with
        it,
Give me yourself, for I see that you belong to me now above
        all, and are folded inseparably together, you love
        and death are,
Nor will I allow you to balk me any more with what I was
        calling life,
For now it is convey'd to me that you are the purports essen-
        tial,
That you hide in these shifting forms of life, for reasons,
        and that they are mainly for you,
That you beyond them come forth to remain, the real reality,
That behind the mask of materials you patiently wait, no
        matter how long,
That you will one day perhaps take control of all,
That you will perhaps dissipate this entire show of appear-
        ance,
That may-be you are what it is all for, but it does not last
        so very long,
But you will last very long.


## WHOEVER YOU ARE HOLDING ME
## NOW IN HAND

Whoever you are holding me now in hand,
Without one thing all will be useless,
I give you fair warning before you attempt me further,
I am not what you supposed, but far different.

Who is he that would become my follower?
Who would sign himself a candidate for my affections?


The way is suspicious, the result uncertain, perhaps destructive,
You would have to give up all else, I alone would expect to be your sole and exclusive standard,
Your novitiate would even then be long and exhausting,
The whole past theory of your life and all conformity to the lives around you would have to be abandon'd,
Therefore release me now before troubling yourself any further, let go your hand from my shoulders,
Put me down and depart on your way.


Or else by stealth in some wood for trial,
Or back of a rock in the open air,
(For in any roof'd room of a house I emerge not, nor in company,
And in libraries I lie as one dumb, a gawk, or unborn, or dead,)
But just possibly with you on a high hill, first watching lest any person for miles around approach unawares,
Or possibly with you sailing at sea, or on the beach of the sea or some quiet island,
Here to put your lips upon mine I permit you,
With the comrade's long-dwelling kiss or the new husband's kiss,
For I am the new husband and I am the comrade.

Or if you will, thrusting me beneath your clothing,
Where I may feel the throbs of your heart or rest upon your
    hip,
Carry me when you go forth over land or sea;
For thus merely touching you is enough, is best,
And thus touching you would I silently sleep and be car-
    ried eternally.


But these leaves conning you con at peril,
For these leaves and me you will not understand,
They will elude you at first and still more afterward, I will
    certainly elude you,
Even while you should think you had unquestionably caught
    me, behold!
Already you see I have escaped from you.


For it is not for what I have put into it that I have written
    this book,
Nor is it by reading it you will acquire it,
Nor do those know me best who admire me and vauntingly
    praise me,
Nor will the candidates for my love (unless at most a very
    few) prove victorious,
Nor will my poems do good only, they will do just as much
    evil, perhaps more,
For all is useless without that which you may guess at many
    times and not hit, that which I hinted at;
Therefore release me and depart on your way.

# FOR YOU O DEMOCRACY

Come, I will make the continent indissoluble,
I will make the most splendid race the sun ever shone upon,
I will make divine magnetic lands,
>With the love of comrades,
>>With the life-long love of comrades.

I will plant companionship thick as trees along all the rivers
>of America, and along the shores of the great lakes,
>and all over the prairies,
I will make inseparable cities with their arms about each
>other's necks,
>By the love of comrades,
>>By the manly love of comrades.

For you these from me, O Democracy, to serve you ma
>femme!
For you, for you I am trilling these songs.

# THESE I SINGING IN SPRING

These I singing in spring collect for lovers,
(For who but I should understand lovers and all their sor-
>row and joy?
And who but I should be the poet of comrades?)
Collecting I traverse the garden the world, but soon I pass
>the gates,

Now along the pond-side, now wading in a little, fearing
	not the wet,
Now by the post-and-rail fences where the old stones thrown
		there, pick'd from the fields, have accumulated,
(Wild-flowers and vines and weeds come up through the
		stones and partly cover them, beyond these I pass,)
Far, far in the forest, or sauntering later in summer, before
		I think where I go,
Solitary, smelling the earthly smell, stopping now and then
		in the silence,
Alone I had thought, yet soon a troop gathers around me,
Some walk by my side and some behind, and some embrace
		my arms or neck,
They the spirits of dear friends dead or alive, thicker they
		come, a great crowd, and I in the middle,
Collecting, dispensing, singing, there I wander with them,
Plucking something for tokens, tossing toward whoever is
		near me,
Here, lilac, with a branch of pine,
Here, out of my pocket, some moss which I pull'd off a live-
		oak in Florida as it hung trailing down,
Here, some pinks and laurel leaves, and a handful of sage,
And here what I now draw from the water, wading in the
		pond-side,
(O here I last saw him that tenderly loves me, and returns
		again never to separate from me,
And this, O this shall henceforth be the token of comrades,
		this calamus-root shall,
Interchange it youths with each other! let none render it
		back!)

And twigs of maple and a bunch of wild orange and chest-
nut,
And stems of currants and plum-blows, and the aromatic
cedar,
These I compass'd around by a thick cloud of spirits,
Wandering, point to or touch as I pass, or throw them
loosely from me,
Indicating to each one what he shall have, giving something
to each;
But what I drew from the water by the pond-side, that I
reserve,
I will give of it, but only to them that love as I myself am
capable of loving.


## NOT HEAVING FROM MY RIBB'D BREAST ONLY

Not heaving from my ribb'd breast only,
Not in sighs at night in rage dissatisfied with myself,
Not in those long-drawn, ill-supprest sighs,
Not in many an oath and promise broken,
Not in my wilful and savage soul's volition,
Not in the subtle nourishment of the air,
Not in this beating and pounding at my temples and wrists,
Not in the curious systole and diastole within which will one
day cease,
Not in many a hungry wish told to the skies only,
Not in cries, laughter, defiances, thrown from me when
alone far in the wilds,
Not in husky pantings through clinch'd teeth,

Not in sounded and resounded words, chattering words,
      echoes, dead words,
Not in the murmurs of my dreams while I sleep,
Nor the other murmurs of these incredible dreams of every
      day,
Nor in the limbs and senses of my body that take you and
      dismiss you continually—not there,
Not in any or all of them O adhesiveness! O pulse of my
      life!
Need I that you exist and show yourself any more than in
      these songs.


## OF THE TERRIBLE DOUBT OF APPEARANCES

Of the terrible doubt of appearances,
Of the uncertainty after all, that we may be deluded,
That may-be reliance and hope are but speculations after all,
That may-be identity beyond the grave is a beautiful fable
      only,
May-be the things I perceive, the animals, plants, men, hills,
      shining and flowing waters,
The skies of day and night, colors, densities, forms, may-be
      these are (as doubtless they are) only apparitions,
      and the real something has yet to be known,
(How often they dart out of themselves as if to confound
      me and mock me!
How often I think neither I know, nor any man knows,
      aught of them,)

May-be seeming to me what they are (as doubtless they
         indeed but seem) as from my present point of view,
         and might prove (as of course they would) nought
         of what they appear, or nought anyhow, from en-
         tirely changed points of view;
To me these and the like of these are curiously answer'd by
         my lovers, my dear friends,
When he whom I love travels with me or sits a long while
         holding me by the hand,
When the subtle air, the impalpable, the sense that words
         and reason hold not, surround us and pervade us,
Then I am charged with untold and untellable wisdom, I am
         silent, I require nothing further,
I cannot answer the question of appearances or that of
         identity beyond the grave,
But I walk or sit indifferent, I am satisfied,
He ahold of my hand has completely satisfied me.

## THE BASE OF ALL METAPHYSICS

And now gentlemen,
A word I give to remain in your memories and minds,
As base and finalè too for all metaphysics.

(So to the students the old professor,
At the close of his crowded course.)

Having studied the new and antique, the Greek and Ger-
         manic systems,

Kant having studied and stated, Fichte and Schelling and
    Hegel,
Stated the lore of Plato, and Socrates greater than Plato,
And greater than Socrates sought and stated, Christ divine
    having studied long,
I see reminiscent to-day those Greek and Germanic systems,
See the philosophies all, Christian churches and tenets see,
Yet underneath Socrates clearly see, and underneath Christ
    the divine I see,
The dear love of man for his comrade, the attraction of
    friend to friend,
Of the well-married husband and wife, of children and
    parents,
Of city for city and land for land.


## RECORDERS AGES HENCE

Recorders ages hence,
Come, I will take you down underneath this impassive ex-
    terior, I will tell you what to say of me,
Publish my name and hang up my picture as that of the
    tenderest lover,
The friend the lover's portrait, of whom his friend his lover
    was fondest,
Who was not proud of his songs, but of the measureless
    ocean of love within him, and freely pour'd it forth,
Who often walk'd lonesome walks thinking of his dear
    friends, his lovers,

Who pensive away from one he lov'd often lay sleepless and dissatisfied at night,
Who knew too well the sick, sick dread lest the one he lov'd might secretly be indifferent to him,
Whose happiest days were far away through fields, in woods, on hills, he and another wandering hand in hand, they twain apart from other men,
Who oft as he saunter'd the streets curv'd with his arm the shoulder of his friend, while the arm of his friend rested upon him also.


## ARE YOU THE NEW PERSON DRAWN TOWARD ME?

Are you the new person drawn toward me?
To begin with take warning, I am surely far different from what you suppose;
Do you suppose you will find in me your ideal?
Do you think it so easy to have me become your lover?
Do you think the friendship of me would be unalloy'd satisfaction?
Do you think I am trusty and faithful?
Do you see no further than this façade, this smooth and tolerant manner of me?
Do you suppose yourself advancing on real ground toward a real heroic man?
Have you no thought O dreamer that it may be all maya, illusion?

# ROOTS AND LEAVES THEMSELVES ALONE

Roots and leaves themselves alone are these,
Scents brought to men and women from the wild woods
        and pond-side,
Breast-sorrel and pinks of love, fingers that wind around
        tighter than vines,
Gushes from the throats of birds hid in the foliage of trees
        as the sun is risen,
Breezes of land and love set from living shores to you on
        the living sea, to you O sailors!
Frost-mellow'd berries and Third-month twigs offer'd fresh
        to young persons wandering out in the fields when
        the winter breaks up,
Love-buds put before you and within you whoever you are,
Buds to be unfolded on the old terms,
If you bring the warmth of the sun to them they will open
        and bring form, color, perfume, to you,
If you become the aliment and the wet they will become
        flowers, fruits, tall branches and trees.

# NOT HEAT FLAMES UP AND CONSUMES

Not heat flames up and consumes,
Not sea-waves hurry in and out,
Not the air delicious and dry, the air of ripe summer, bears
        lightly along white down-balls of myriads of seeds,
Wafted, sailing gracefully, to drop where they may;

Not these, O none of these more than the flames of me,
    consuming, burning for his love whom I love,
O none more than I hurrying in and out;
Does the tide hurry, seeking something, and never give up?
    O I the same,
O nor down-balls nor perfumes, nor the high rain-emitting
    clouds, are borne through the open air,
Any more than my soul is borne through the open air,
Wafted in all directions O love, for friendship, for you.


## TRICKLE DROPS

Trickle drops! my blue veins leaving!
O drops of me! trickle, slow drops,
Candid from me falling, drip, bleeding drops,
From wounds made to free you whence you were prison'd,
From my face, from my forehead and lips,
From my breast, from within where I was conceal'd, press
    forth red drops, confession drops,
Stain every page, stain every song I sing, every word I say,
    bloody drops,
Let them know your scarlet heat, let them glisten,
Saturate them with yourself all ashamed and wet,
Glow upon all I have written or shall write, bleeding drops,
Let it all be seen in your light, blushing drops.

# CITY OF ORGIES

City of orgies, walks and joys,
City whom that I have lived and sung in your midst will one
        day make you illustrious,
Not the pageants of you, not your shifting tableaus, your
        spectacles, repay me,
Not the interminable rows of your houses, nor the ships at
        the wharves,
Nor the processions in the streets, nor the bright windows
        with goods in them,
Nor to converse with learn'd persons, or bear my share in
        the soiree or feast;
Not those, but as I pass O Manhattan, your frequent and
        swift flash of eyes offering me love,
Offering response to my own—these repay me,
Lovers, continual lovers, only repay me.


# TO A STRANGER

Passing stranger! you do not know how longingly I look
        upon you,
You must be he I was seeking, or she I was seeking, (it
        comes to me as of a dream,)
I have somewhere surely lived a life of joy with you,
All is recall'd as we flit by each other, fluid, affectionate,
        chaste, matured,

You grew up with me, were a boy with me or a girl with
    me,
I ate with you and slept with you, your body has become not
    yours only nor left my body mine only,
You give me the pleasure of your eyes, face, flesh, as we
    pass, you take of my beard, breast, hands, in return,
I am not to speak to you, I am to think of you when I sit
    alone or wake at night alone,
I am to wait, I do not doubt I am to meet you again,
I am to see to it that I do not lose you.


## THIS MOMENT YEARNING AND THOUGHTFUL

This moment yearning and thoughtful sitting alone,
It seems to me there are other men in other lands yearning
    and thoughtful,
It seems to me I can look over and behold them in Germany,
    Italy, France, Spain,
Or far, far away, in China, or in Russia or Japan, talking
    other dialects,
And it seems to me if I could know those men I should be-
    come attached to them as I do to men in my own
    lands,
O I know we should be brethren and lovers,
I know I should be happy with them.

# I HEAR IT WAS CHARGED AGAINST ME

I hear it was charged against me that I sought to destroy
    institutions,
But really I am neither for nor against institutions,
(What indeed have I in common with them? or what with
    the destruction of them?)
Only I will establish in the Mannahatta and in every city of
    these States inland and seaboard,
And in the fields and woods, and above every keel little or
    large that dents the water,
Without edifices or rules or trustees or any argument,
The institution of the dear love of comrades.


# THE PRAIRIE-GRASS DIVIDING

The prairie-grass dividing, its special odor breathing,
I demand of it the spiritual corresponding,
Demand the most copious and close companionship of men,
Demand the blades to rise of words, acts, beings,
Those of the open atmosphere, coarse, sunlit, fresh, nutri-
    tious,
Those that go their own gait, erect, stepping with freedom
    and command, leading not following,
Those with a never-quell'd audacity, those with sweet and
    lusty flesh clear of taint,
Those that look carelessly in the faces of Presidents and gov-
    ernors, as to say *Who are you?*

Those of earth-born passion, simple, never constrain'd,
  never obedient,
Those of inland America.


## WHEN I PERUSE THE CONQUER'D FAME

When I peruse the conquer'd fame of heroes and the vic-
  tories of mighty generals, I do not envy the gen-
  erals,
Nor the President in his Presidency, nor the rich in his great
  house,
But when I hear of the brotherhood of lovers, how it was
  with them,
How together through life, through dangers, odium, un-
  changing, long and long,
Through youth and through middle and old age, how un-
  faltering, how affectionate and faithful they were,
Then I am pensive—I hastily walk away fill'd with the bit-
  terest envy.


## A PROMISE TO CALIFORNIA

A promise to California,
Or inland to the great pastoral Plains, and on to Puget sound
  and Oregon;
Sojourning east a while longer, soon I travel toward you,
  to remain, to teach robust American love,

For I know very well that I and robust love belong among
      you, inland, and along the Western sea;
For these States tend inland and toward the Western sea,
      and I will also.


## HERE THE FRAILEST LEAVES OF ME

Here the frailest leaves of me and yet my strongest lasting,
Here I shade and hide my thoughts, I myself do not expose
      them,
And yet they expose me more than all my other poems.


## NO LABOR-SAVING MACHINE

No labor-saving machine,
Nor discovery have I made,
Nor will I be able to leave behind me any wealthy bequest
      to found a hospital or library,
Nor reminiscence of any deed of courage for America,
Nor literary success nor intellect, nor book for the book-
      shelf,
But a few carols vibrating through the air I leave,
For comrades and lovers.

# A LEAF FOR HAND IN HAND

A leaf for hand in hand;
You natural persons old and young!
You on the Mississippi and on all the branches and bayous
of the Mississippi!
You friendly boatmen and mechanics! you roughs!
You twain! and all processions moving along the streets!
I wish to infuse myself among you till I see it common for
you to walk hand in hand.


# EARTH, MY LIKENESS

Earth, my likeness,
Though you look so impassive, ample and spheric there,
I now suspect that is not all;
I now suspect there is something fierce in you eligible to
burst forth,
For an athlete is enamour'd of me, and I of him,
But toward him there is something fierce and terrible in me
eligible to burst forth,
I dare not tell it in words, not even in these songs.


# I DREAM'D IN A DREAM

I dream'd in a dream I saw a city invincible to the attacks of
the whole of the rest of the earth,
I dream'd that was the new city of Friends,

Nothing was greater there than the quality of robust love, it
      led the rest,
It was seen every hour in the actions of the men of that city,
And in all their looks and words.


## TO THE EAST AND TO THE WEST

To the East and to the West,
To the man of the Seaside State and of Pennsylvania,
To the Kanadian of the north, to the Southerner I love,
These with perfect trust to depict you as myself, the germs
      are in all men,
I believe the main purport of these States is to found a
      superb friendship, exaltè, previously unknown,
Because I perceive it waits, and has been always waiting,
      latent in all men.


## SOMETIMES WITH ONE I LOVE

Sometimes with one I love I fill myself with rage for fear I
      effuse unreturn'd love,
But now I think there is no unreturn'd love, the pay is cer-
      tain one way or another,
(I loved a certain person ardently and my love was not re-
      turn'd,
Yet out of that I have written these songs.)

# FAST ANCHOR'D ETERNAL O LOVE!

Fast-anchor'd eternal O love! O woman I love!
O bride! O wife! more resistless than I can tell, the thought
     of you!
Then separate, as disembodied or another born,
Ethereal, the last athletic reality, my consolation,
I ascend, I float in the regions of your love O man,
O sharer of my roving life.


## AMONG THE MULTITUDE

Among the men and women the multitude,
I perceive one picking me out by secret and divine signs,
Acknowledging none else, not parent, wife, husband,
     brother, child, any nearer than I am,
Some are baffled, but that one is not—that one knows me.

Ah lover and perfect equal,
I meant that you should discover me so by faint indirections,
And I when I meet you mean to discover you by the like
     in you.


## FULL OF LIFE NOW

Full of life now, compact, visible,
I, forty years old the eighty-third year of the States,
To one a century hence or any number of centuries hence,
To you yet unborn these, seeking you.

When you read these I that was visible am become invisible,

Now it is you, compact, visible, realizing my poems, seeking
      me,

Fancying how happy you were if I could be with you and
      become your comrade;

Be it as if I were with you. (Be not too certain but I am now
      with you.)

# Song of the Open Road

I

Afoot and light-hearted I take to the open road,
Healthy, free, the world before me,
The long brown path before me leading wherever I choose.

Henceforth I ask not good-fortune, I myself am good-
fortune,
Henceforth I whimper no more, postpone no more, need
nothing,
Done with indoor complaints, libraries, querulous criti-
cisms,
Strong and content I travel the open road.

The earth, that is sufficient,
I do not want the constellations any nearer,
I know they are very well where they are,
I know they suffice for those who belong to them.

(Still here I carry my old delicious burdens,
I carry them, men and women, I carry them with me wher-
ever I go,

I swear it is impossible for me to get rid of them,
I am fill'd with them, and I will fill them in return.)


2

You road I enter upon and look around, I believe you are
      not all that is here,
I believe that much unseen is also here.


Here the profound lesson of reception, nor preference nor
      denial,
The black with his woolly head, the felon, the diseas'd, the
      illiterate person, are not denied;
The birth, the hasting after the physician, the beggar's
      tramp, the drunkard's stagger, the laughing party
      of mechanics,
The escaped youth, the rich person's carriage, the fop, the
      eloping couple,
The early market-man, the hearse, the moving of furniture
      into the town, the return back from the town,
They pass, I also pass, any thing passes, none can be inter-
      dicted,
None but are accepted, none but shall be dear to me.


3

You air that serves me with breath to speak!
You objects that call from diffusion my meanings and give
      them shape!

You light that wraps me and all things in delicate equable
    showers!
You paths worn in the irregular hollows by the roadsides!
I believe you are latent with unseen existences, you are so
    dear to me.


You flagg'd walks of the cities! you strong curbs at the edges!
You ferries! you planks and posts of wharves! you timber-
    lined sides! you distant ships!
You rows of houses! you window-pierc'd façades! you roofs!
You porches and entrances! you copings and iron guards!
You windows whose transparent shells might expose so
    much!
You doors and ascending steps! you arches!
You gray stones of interminable pavements! you trodden
    crossings!
From all that has touch'd you I believe you have imparted
    to yourselves, and now would impart the same se-
    cretly to me,
From the living and the dead you have peopled your im-
    passive surfaces, and the spirits thereof would be
    evident and amicable with me.


4


The earth expanding right hand and left hand,
The picture alive, every part in its best light,
The music falling in where it is wanted, and stopping where
    it is not wanted,

The cheerful voice of the public road, the gay fresh senti-
    ment of the road.

O highway I travel, do you say to me *Do not leave me?*
Do you say *Venture not—if you leave me you are lost?*
Do you say *I am already prepared, I am well-beaten and un-
    denied, adhere to me?*

O public road, I say back I am not afraid to leave you, yet
    I love you,
You express me better than I can express myself,
You shall be more to me than my poem.

I think heroic deeds were all conceiv'd in the open air, and
    all free poems also,
I think I could stop here myself and do miracles,
I think whatever I shall meet on the road I shall like, and
    whoever beholds me shall like me,
I think whoever I see must be happy.

5

From this hour I ordain myself loos'd of limits and imag-
    inary lines,
Going where I list, my own master total and absolute,
Listening to others, considering well what they say,
Pausing, searching, receiving, contemplating,
Gently, but with undeniable will, divesting myself of the
    holds that would hold me.

145

I inhale great draughts of space,
The east and the west are mine, and the north and the south
    are mine.


I am larger, better than I thought,
I did not know I held so much goodness.


All seems beautiful to me,
I can repeat over to men and women You have done such
        good to me I would do the same to you,
I will recruit for myself and you as I go,
I will scatter myself among men and women as I go,
I will toss a new gladness and roughness among them,
Whoever denies me it shall not trouble me,
Whoever accepts me he or she shall be blessed and shall
        bless me.


6


Now if a thousand perfect men were to appear it would not
        amaze me,
Now if a thousand beautiful forms of women appear'd it
        would not astonish me.


Now I see the secret of the making of the best persons,
It is to grow in the open air and to eat and sleep with the
        earth.

Here a great personal deed has room,
(Such a deed seizes upon the hearts of the whole race of
        men,
Its effusion of strength and will overwhelms law and mocks
        all authority and all argument against it.)


Here is the test of wisdom,
Wisdom is not finally tested in schools,
Wisdom cannot be pass'd from one having it to another not
        having it,
Wisdom is of the soul, is not susceptible of proof, is its own
        proof,
Applies to all stages and objects and qualities and is content,
Is the certainty of the reality and immortality of things, and
        the excellence of things;
Something there is in the float of the sight of things that pro-
        vokes it out of the soul.


Now I re-examine philosophies and religions,
They may prove well in lecture-rooms, yet not prove at all
        under the spacious clouds and along the landscape
        and flowing currents.


Here is realization,
Here is a man tallied—he realizes here what he has in him,
The past, the future, majesty, love—if they are vacant of
        you, you are vacant of them.


Only the kernel of every object nourishes;
Where is he who tears off the husks for you and me?

Where is he that undoes stratagems and envelopes for you
      and me?

Here is adhesiveness, it is not previously fashion'd, it is
      apropos;
Do you know what it is as you pass to be loved by strangers?
Do you know the talk of those turning eye-balls?


## 7

Here is the efflux of the soul,
The efflux of the soul comes from within through embow-
      er'd gates, ever provoking questions,
These yearnings why are they? these thoughts in the dark-
      ness why are they?
Why are there men and women that while they are nigh
      me the sunlight expands my blood?
Why when they leave me do my pennants of joy sink flat
      and lank?
Why are there trees I never walk under but large and
      melodious thoughts descend upon me?
(I think they hang there winter and summer on those trees
      and always drop fruit as I pass;)
What is it I interchange so suddenly with strangers?
What with some driver as I ride on the seat by his side?
What with some fisherman drawing his seine by the shore
      as I walk by and pause?
What gives me to be free to a woman's and man's good-
      will? what gives them to be free to mine?

8

The efflux of the soul is happiness, here is happiness,
I think it pervades the open air, waiting at all times,
Now it flows unto us, we are rightly charged.

Here rises the fluid and attaching character,
The fluid and attaching character is the freshness and sweet-
            ness of man and woman,
(The herbs of the morning sprout no fresher and sweeter
            every day out of the roots of themselves, than it
            sprouts fresh and sweet continually out of itself.)

Toward the fluid and attaching character exudes the sweat
            of the love of young and old,
From it falls distill'd the charm that mocks beauty and
            attainments,
Toward it heaves the shuddering longing ache of contact.

9

Allons! whoever you are come travel with me!
Traveling with me you find what never tires.

The earth never tires,
The earth is rude, silent, incomprehensible at first, Nature
            is rude and incomprehensible at first,
Be not discouraged, keep on, there are divine things well
            envelop'd,

49

I swear to you there are divine things more beautiful than
    words can tell.

Allons! we must not stop here,
However sweet these laid-up stores, however convenient
    this dwelling we cannot remain here,
However shelter'd this port and however calm these waters
    we must not anchor here,
However welcome the hospitality that surrounds us we are
    permitted to receive it but a little while.


10

Allons! the inducements shall be greater,
We will sail pathless and wild seas,
We will go where winds blow, waves dash, and the Yankee
    clipper speeds by under full sail.

Allons! with power, liberty, the earth, the elements,
Health, defiance, gayety, self-esteem, curiosity;
Allons! from all formules!
From your formules, O bat-eyed and materialistic priests.

The stale cadaver blocks up the passage—the burial waits
    no longer.

Allons! yet take warning!
He traveling with me needs the best blood, thews, endur-
    ance,

None may come to the trial till he or she bring courage
and health,
Come not here if you have already spent the best of your-
self,
Only those may come who come in sweet and determin'd
bodies,
No diseas'd person, no rum-drinker or venereal taint is per-
mitted here.


(I and mine do not convince by arguments, similes, rhymes,
We convince by our presence.)


## 11

Listen! I will be honest with you,
I do not offer the old smooth prizes, but offer rough new
prizes,
These are the days that must happen to you:
You shall not heap up what is call'd riches,
You shall scatter with lavish hand all that you earn or
achieve,
You but arrive at the city to which you were destin'd, you
hardly settle yourself to satisfaction before you are
call'd by an irresistible call to depart,
You shall be treated to the ironical smiles and mockings of
those who remain behind you,
What beckonings of love you receive you shall only answer
with passionate kisses of parting,

You shall not allow the hold of those who spread their
reach'd hands toward you.

12

Allons! after the great Companions, and to belong to them!
They too are on the road—they are the swift and majestic
men—they are the greatest women,
Enjoyers of calms of seas and storms of seas,
Sailors of many a ship, walkers of many a mile of land,
Habituès of many distant countries, habituès of far-distant
dwellings,
Trusters of men and women, observers of cities, solitary
toilers,
Pausers and contemplators of tufts, blossoms, shells of the
shore,
Dancers at wedding-dances, kissers of brides, tender help-
ers of children, bearers of children,
Soldiers of revolts, standers by gaping graves, lowerers-
down of coffins,
Journeyers over consecutive seasons, over the years, the
curious years each emerging from that which pre-
ceded it,
Journeyers as with companions, namely their own diverse
phases,
Fourth-steppers from the latent unrealized baby-days,
Journeyers gayly with their own youth, journeyers with
their bearded and well-gain'd manhood,

Journeyers with their womanhood, ample, unsurpass'd,
content,
Journeyers with their own sublime old age of manhood
or womanhood,
Old age, calm, expanded, broad with the haughty breadth
of the universe,
Old age, flowing free with the delicious near-by freedom
of death.


## 13

Allons! to that which is endless as it was beginningless,
To undergo much, tramps of days, rests of nights,
To emerge all in the travel they tend to, and the days and
nights they tend to,
Again to merge them in the start of superior journeys,
To see nothing anywhere but what you may reach it and
pass it,
To conceive no time, however distant, but what you may
reach it and pass it,
To look up or down no road but it stretches and waits for
you, however long but it stretches and waits for
you,
To see no being, not God's or any, but you also go thither,
To see no possession but you may possess it, enjoying all
without labor or purchase, abstracting the feast yet
not abstracting one particle of it,
To take the best of the farmer's farm and the rich man's
elegant villa, and the chaste blessings of the well-

married couple, and the fruits of orchards and
flowers of gardens,
To take to your use out of the compact cities as you pass
through,
To carry buildings and streets with you afterward wherever
you go,
To gather the minds of men out of their brains as you en-
counter them, to gather the love out of their hearts,
To take your lovers on the road with you, for all that you
leave them behind you,
To know the universe itself as a road, as many roads, as
roads for traveling souls.


All parts away for the progress of souls,
All religion, all solid things, arts, governments—all that
was or is apparent upon this globe or any globe, falls
into niches and corners before the procession of
souls along the grand roads of the universe.


Of the progress of the souls of men and women along the
grand roads of the universe, all other progress is
the needed emblem and sustenance.


Forever alive, forever forward,
Stately, solemn, sad, withdrawn, baffled, mad, turbulent,
feeble, dissatisfied,
Desperate, proud, fond, sick, accepted by men, rejected by
men,

They go! they go! I know that they go, but I know not
     where they go,
But I know that they go toward the best—toward some-
     thing great.


Whoever you are, come forth! or man or woman come
     forth!
You must not stay sleeping and dallying there in the house,
     though you built it, or though it has been built for
     you.


Out of the dark confinement! out from behind the screen!
It is useless to protest, I know all and expose it.


Behold through you as bad as the rest,
Through the laughter, dancing, dining, supping, of people,
Inside of dresses and ornaments, inside of those wash'd
     and trimm'd faces,
Behold a secret silent loathing and despair.


No husband, no wife, no friend, trusted to hear the con-
     fession,
Another self, a duplicate of every one, skulking and hid-
     ing it goes,
Formless and wordless through the streets of the cities,
     polite and bland in the parlors,
In the cars of railroads, in steamboats, in the public as-
     sembly,

Home to the houses of men and women, at the table, in
the bedroom, everywhere,
Smartly attired, countenance smiling, form upright, death
under the breast-bones, hell under the skull-bones,
Under the broadcloth and gloves, under the ribbons and
artificial flowers,
Keeping fair with the customs, speaking not a syllable of
itself,
Speaking of any thing else but never of itself.


14

Allons! through struggles and wars!
The goal that was named cannot be countermanded.


Have the past struggles succeeded?
What has succeeded? yourself? your nation? Nature?
Now understand me well—it is provided in the essence of
things that from any fruition of success, no matter
what, shall come forth something to make a greater
struggle necessary.


My call is the call of battle, I nourish active rebellion,
He going with me must go well arm'd,
He going with me goes often with spare diet, poverty, angry
enemies, desertions.

## 15

Allons! the road is before us!
It is safe—I have tried it—my own feet have tried it well—
    —be not detain'd!
Let the paper remain on the desk unwritten, and the book
        on the shelf unopen'd!
Let the tools remain in the workshop! let the money remain
        unearn'd!
Let the school stand! mind not the cry of the teacher!
Let the preacher preach in his pulpit! let the lawyer plead
        in the court, and the judge expound the law.

Camerado, I give you my hand!
I give you my love more precious than money,
I give you myself before preaching or law;
Will you give me yourself? will you come travel with me?
Shall we stick by each other as long as we live?

# Crossing Brooklyn Ferry

Flood-tide below me! I see you face to face!
Clouds of the west—sun there half an hour high—I see
      you also face to face.

Crowds of men and women attired in the usual costume,
      how curious you are to me!
On the ferry-boats the hundreds and hundreds that cross,
      returning home, are more curious to me than you
      suppose,
And you that shall cross from shore to shore years hence are
      more to me, and more in my meditations, than you
      might suppose.

The impalpable sustenance of me from all things at all
      hours of the day,
The simple, compact, well-join'd scheme, myself disinte-
      grated, every one disintegrated yet part of the
      scheme,

The similitudes of the past and those of the future,
The glories strung like beads on my smallest sights and
          hearings, on the walk in the street and the passage
          over the river,
The current rushing so swiftly and swimming with me far
          away,
The others that are to follow me, the ties between me and
          them,
The certainty of others, the life, love, sight, hearing of
          others.


Others will enter the gates of the ferry and cross from
          shore to shore,
Others will watch the run of the flood-tide,
Others will see the shipping of Manhattan north and west,
          and the heights of Brooklyn to the south and east,
Others will see the islands large and small;
Fifty years hence, others will see them as they cross, the
          sun half an hour high,
A hundred years hence, or ever so many hundred years
          hence, others will see them,
Will enjoy the sunset, the pouring-in of the flood-tide, the
          falling-back to the sea of the ebb-tide.


### 3

It avails not, time nor place—distance avails not,
I am with you, you men and women of a generation, or ever
          so many generations hence,

Just as you feel when you look on the river and sky, so I felt,
Just as any of you is one of a living crowd, I was one of a
crowd,
Just as you are refresh'd by the gladness of the river and
the bright flow, I was refresh'd,
Just as you stand and lean on the rail, yet hurry with the
swift current, I stood yet was hurried,
Just as you look on the numberless masts of ships and the
thick-stemm'd pipes of steamboats, I look'd.


I too many and many a time cross'd the river of old,
Watched the Twelfth-month sea-gulls, saw them high in
the air floating with motionless wings, oscillating
their bodies,
Saw how the glistening yellow lit up parts of their bodies
and left the rest in strong shadow,
Saw the slow-wheeling circles and the gradual edging
toward the south,
Saw the reflection of the summer sky in the water,
Had my eyes dazzled by the shimmering track of beams,
Look'd at the fine centrifugal spokes of light round the
shape of my head in the sunlit water,
Look'd on the haze on the hills southward and south-west-
ward,
Look'd on the vapor as it flew in fleeces tinged with violet,
Look'd toward the lower bay to notice the vessels arriving,
Saw their approach, saw aboard those that were near me,
Saw the white sails of schooners and sloops, saw the ships
at anchor,

The sailors at work in the rigging or out astride the spars,

The round masts, the swinging motion of the hulls, the
　　　slender serpentine pennants,

The large and small steamers in motion, the pilots in their
　　　pilot-houses,

The white wake left by the passage, the quick tremulous
　　　whirl of the wheels,

The flags of all nations, the falling of them at sunset,

The scallop-edged waves in the twilight, the ladled cups,
　　　the frolicsome crests and glistening,

The stretch afar growing dimmer and dimmer, the gray
　　　walls of the granite storehouses by the docks,

On the river the shadowy group, the big steam-tug closely
　　　flank'd on each side by the barges, the hay-boat, the
　　　belated lighter,

On the neighboring shore the fires from the foundry chim-
　　　neys burning high and glaringly into the night,

Casting their flicker of black contrasted with wild red and
　　　yellow light over the tops of houses, and down into
　　　the clefts of streets.


4


These and all else were to me the same as they are to you,

I loved well those cities, loved well the stately and rapid
　　　river,

The men and women I saw were all near to me,

Others the same—others who look back on me because I
    look'd forward to them,
(The time will come, though I stop here to-day and to-
    night.)


5

What is it then between us?
What is the count of the scores or hundreds of years between
    us?


Whatever it is, it avails not—distance avails not, and place
    avails not,
I too lived, Brooklyn of ample hills was mine,
I too walk'd the streets of Manhattan island, and bathed
    in the waters around it,
I too felt the curious abrupt questionings stir within me,
In the day among crowds of people sometimes they came
    upon me,
In my walks home late at night or as I lay in my bed they
    came upon me,
I too had been struck from the float forever held in solution,
I too had receiv'd identity by my body,
That I was I knew was of my body, and what I should be
    I knew I should be of my body.

It is not upon you alone the dark patches fall,
The dark threw its patches down upon me also,
The best I had done seem'd to me blank and suspicious,
My great thoughts as I supposed them, were they not in
      reality meagre?
Nor is it you alone who know what it is to be evil,
I am he who knew what it was to be evil,
I too knitted the old knot of contrariety,
Blabb'd, blush'd, resented, lied, stole, grudg'd,
Had guile, anger, lust, hot wishes I dared not speak,
Was wayward, vain, greedy, shallow, sly, cowardly, ma-
      lignant,
The wolf, the snake, the hog, not wanting in me,
The cheating look, the frivolous word, the adulterous wish,
      not wanting,
Refusals, hates, postponements, meanness, laziness, none
      of these wanting,
Was one with the rest, the days and haps of the rest,
Was call'd by my nighest name by clear loud voices of
      young men as they saw me approaching or passing,
Felt their arms on my neck as I stood, or the negligent lean-
      ing of their flesh against me as I sat,
Saw many I loved in the street or ferry-boat or public
      assembly, yet never told them a word,
Lived the same life with the rest, the same old laughing,
      gnawing, sleeping,
Play'd the part that still looks back on the actor or actress,

The same old role, the role that is what we make it, as great
　　　as we like,
Or as small as we like, or both great and small.


# 7

Closer yet I approach you,
What thought you have of me now, I had as much of you—
　　　I laid in my stores in advance,
I consider'd long and seriously of you before you were born.


Who was to know what should come home to me?
Who knows but I am enjoying this?
Who knows, for all the distance, but I am as good as look-
　　　ing at you now, for all you cannot see me?


# 8

Ah, what can ever be more stately and admirable to me
　　　than mast-hemm'd Manhattan?
River and sunset and scallop-edg'd waves of flood-tide?
The sea-gulls oscillating their bodies, the hay-boat in the
　　　twilight, and the belated lighter?
What gods can exceed these that clasp me by the hand, and
　　　with voices I love call me promptly and loudly by
　　　my nighest name as I approach?
What is more subtle than this which ties me to the woman
　　　or man that looks in my face?

Which fuses me into you now, and pours my meaning into
 you?

We understand then do we not?
What I promis'd without mentioning it, have you not ac-
 cepted?
What the study could not teach—what the preaching could
 not accomplish is accomplish'd, is it not?


## 9

Flow on, river! flow with the flood-tide, and ebb with the
 ebb-tide!
Frolic on, crested and scallop-edg'd waves!
Gorgeous clouds of the sunset! drench with your splendor
 me, or the men and women generations after me!
Cross from shore to shore, countless crowds of passengers!
Stand up, tall masts of Mannahatta! stand up, beautiful hills
 of Brooklyn!
Throb, baffled and curious brain! throw out questions and
 answers!
Suspend here and everywhere, eternal float of solution!
Gaze, loving and thirsting eyes, in the house or street or
 public assembly!
Sound out, voices of young men! loudly and musically call
 me by my nighest name!
Live, old life! play the part that looks back on the actor
 or actress!

Play the old role, the role that is great or small according
        as one makes it!

Consider, you who peruse me, whether I may not in un-
        known ways be looking upon you;

Be firm, rail over the river, to support those who lean idly,
        yet haste with the hasting current;

Fly on, sea-birds! fly sideways, or wheel in large circles high
        in the air;

Receive the summer sky, you water, and faithfully hold it
        till all downcast eyes have time to take it from you!

Diverge, fine spokes of light, from the shape of my head,
        or any one's head, in the sunlit water!

Come on, ships from the lower bay! pass up or down, white-
        sail'd schooners, sloops, lighters!

Flaunt away, flags of all nations! be duly lower'd at sunset!

Burn high your fires, foundry chimneys! cast black shadows
        at nightfall! cast red and yellow light over the tops
        of the houses!

Appearances, now or henceforth, indicate what you are,

You necessary film, continue to envelop the soul,

About my body for me, and your body for you, be hung our
        divinest aromas,

Thrive, cities—bring your freight, bring your shows, ample
        and sufficient rivers,

Expand, being than which none else is perhaps more spirit-
        ual,

Keep your places, objects than which none else is more
        lasting.

You have waited, you always wait, you dumb, beautiful
  ministers,
We receive you with free sense at last, and are insatiate
  henceforward,
Not you any more shall be able to foil us, or withhold your-
  selves from us,
We use you, and do not cast you aside—we plant you perma-
  nently within us,
We fathom you not—we love you—there is perfection in
  you also,
You furnish your parts toward eternity,
Great or small, you furnish your parts toward the soul.

# Song of the Answerer

Now list to my morning's romanza, I tell the signs of the
 Answerer,
To the cities and farms I sing as they spread in the sunshine
 before me.


A young man comes to me bearing a message from his
 brother,
How shall the young man know the whether and when of
 his brother?
Tell him to send me the signs.


And I stand before the young man face to face, and take
 his right hand in my left hand and his left hand in
 my right hand,
And I answer for his brother and for men, and I answer
 for him that answers for all, and send these signs.


Him all wait for, him all yield up to, his word is decisive
 and final,

Him they accept, in him lave, in him perceive themselves
    as amid light,
Him they immerse and he immerses them.


Beautiful women, the haughtiest nations, laws, the land-
    scape, people, animals,
The profound earth and its attributes and the unquiet ocean,
    (so tell I my morning's romanza,)
All enjoyments and properties and money, and whatever
    money will buy,
The best farms, others toiling and planting and he unavoid-
    ably reaps,
The noblest and costliest cities, others grading and building
    and he domiciles there,
Nothing for any one but what is for him, near and far are
    for him, the ships in the offing,
The perpetual shows and marches on land are for him if
    they are for anybody.


He puts things in their attitudes,
He puts to-day out of himself with plasticity and love,
He places his own times, reminiscences, parents, brothers
    and sisters, associations, employment, politics, so
    that the rest never shame them afterward, nor as-
    sume to command them.


He is the Answerer,
What can be answer'd he answers, and what cannot be
    answer'd he shows how it cannot be answer'd.

A man is a summons and challenge,
(It is vain to skulk—do you hear that mocking and laughter?
   do you hear the ironical echoes?)

Books, friendships, philosophers, priests, action, pleasure,
   pride, beat up and down seeking to give satisfaction,
He indicates the satisfaction, and indicates them that beat
   up and down also.

Whichever the sex, whatever the season or place, he may
   go freshly and gently and safely by day or by night,
He has the pass-key of hearts, to him the response of the
   prying of hands on the knobs.

His welcome is universal, the flow of beauty is not more
   welcome or universal than he is,
The person he favors by day or sleeps with at night is
   blessed.

Every existence has its idiom, every thing has an idiom and
   tongue,
He resolves all tongues into his own and bestows it upon
   men, and any man translates, and any man trans-
   lates himself also,
One part does not counteract another part, he is the joiner,
   he sees how they join.

He says indifferently and alike *How are you friend?* to the
   President at his levee,

And he says *Good-day my brother,* to Cudge that hoes in
       the sugar-field,
And both understand him and know that his speech is
       right.


He walks with perfect ease in the capitol,
He walks among the Congress, and one Representative
       says to another, *Here is our equal appearing and
       new.*


Then the mechanics take him for a mechanic,
And the soldiers suppose him to be a soldier, and the
       sailors that he has follow'd the sea,
And the authors take him for an author, and the artists for
       an artist,
And the laborers perceive he could labor with them and love
       them,
No matter what the work is, that he is the one to follow it
       or has follow'd it,
No matter what the nation, that he might find his brothers
       and sisters there.


The English believe he comes of their English stock,
A Jew to the Jew he seems, a Russ to the Russ, usual and
       near, removed from none.


Whoever he looks at in the traveler's coffee-house claims
       him,

The Italian or Frenchman is sure, the German is sure, the
    Spaniard is sure, and the island Cuban is sure,
The engineer, the deck-hand on the great lakes, or on the
    Mississippi or St. Lawrence or Sacramento, or Hud-
    son or Paumanok sound, claims him.


The gentleman of perfect blood acknowledges his perfect
    blood,
The insulter, the prostitute, the angry person, the beggar,
    see themselves in the ways of him, he strangely
    transmutes them,
They are not vile any more, they hardly know themselves
    they are so grown.


2

The indications and tally of time,
Perfect sanity shows the master among philosophs,
Time, always without break, indicates itself in parts
What always indicates the poet is the crowd of the pleasant
    company of singers, and their words,
The words of the singers are the hours or minutes of the
    light or dark, but the words of the maker of poems
    are the general light and dark,
The maker of poems settles justice, reality, immortality,
His insight and power encircle things and the human race,
He is the glory and extract thus far of things and of the
    human race.

The singers do not beget, only the Poet begets,
The singers are welcom'd, understood, appear often enough,
      but rare has the day been, likewise the spot, of the
      birth of the maker of poems, the Answerer,
(Not every century nor every five centuries has contain'd
      such a day, for all its names.)

The singers of successive hours of centuries may have
      ostensible names, but the name of each of them is
      one of the singers,
The name of each is, eye-singer, ear-singer, head-singer,
      sweet-singer, night-singer, parlor-singer, love-
      singer, weird-singer, or something else.

All this time and at all times wait the words of true poems,
The words of true poems do not merely please,
The true poets are not followers of beauty but the august
      masters of beauty;
The greatness of sons is the exuding of the greatness of
      mothers and fathers,
The words of true poems are the tuft and final applause of
      science.

Divine instinct, breadth of vision, the law of reason, health,
      rudeness of body, withdrawnness,
Gayety, sun-tan, air-sweetness, such are some of the words
      of poems.

The sailor and traveler underlie the maker of poems, the
      Answerer,

The builder, geometer, chemist, anatomist, phrenologist,
        artist, all these underlie the maker of poems, the
        Answerer.


The words of the true poems give you more than poems,
They give you to form for yourself poems, religions, politics,
        war, peace, behavior, histories, essays, daily life, and
        every thing else,
They balance ranks, colors, races, creeds, and the sexes,
They do not seek beauty, they are sought,
Forever touching them or close upon them follows beauty,
        longing, fain, love-sick.


They prepare for death, yet are they not the finish, but
        rather the outset,
They bring none to his or her terminus or to be content and
        full,
Whom they take they take into space to behold the birth
        of stars, to learn one of the meanings,
To launch off with absolute faith, to sweep through the
        ceaseless rings and never be quiet again.

# Song of the Broad-Axe

Weapon shapely, naked, wan,
Head from the mother's bowels drawn,
Wooded flesh and metal bone, limb only one and lip only
      one,
Gray-blue leaf by red-heat grown, helve produced from a
      little seed sown,
Resting the grass amid and upon,
To be lean'd and to lean on.

Strong shapes and attributes of strong shapes, masculine
      trades, sights and sounds,
Long varied train of an emblem, dabs of music,
Fingers of the organist skipping staccato over the keys
      of the great organ.

2

Welcome are all earth's lands, each for its kind,
Welcome are lands of pine and oak,
Welcome are lands of the lemon and fig,

Welcome are lands of gold,
Welcome are lands of wheat and maize, welcome those of
      the grape,
Welcome are lands of sugar and rice,
Welcome the cotton-lands, welcome those of the white
      potato and sweet potato,
Welcome are mountains, flats, sands, forests, prairies,
Welcome the rich borders of rivers, table-lands, openings,
Welcome the measureless grazing-lands, welcome the teem-
      ing soil of orchards, flax, honey, hemp;
Welcome just as much the other more hard-faced lands,
Lands rich as lands of gold or wheat and fruit lands,
Lands of mines, lands of the manly and rugged ores,
Lands of coal, copper, lead, tin, zinc,
Lands of iron—lands of the make of the axe.


3

The log at the wood-pile, the axe supported by it,
The sylvan hut, the vine over the doorway, the space clear'd
      for a garden,
The irregular tapping of rain down on the leaves after the
      storm is lull'd,
The wailing and moaning at intervals, the thought of the
      sea,
The thought of ships struck in the storm and put on their
      beam ends, and the cutting away of masts,
The sentiment of the huge timbers of old-fashion'd houses
      and barns,

The remember'd print or narrative, the voyage at a venture
     of men, families, goods,
The disembarkation, the founding of a new city,
The voyage of those who sought a New England and found
     it, the outset anywhere,
The settlements of the Arkansas, Colorado, Ottawa, Wil-
     lamette,
The slow progress, the scant fare, the axe, rifle, saddle-
     bags;
The beauty of all adventurous and daring persons,
The beauty of wood-boys and wood-men with their clear
     untrimm'd faces,
The beauty of independence, departure, actions that rely on
     themselves,
The American contempt for statutes and ceremonies, the
     boundless impatience of restraint,
The loose drift of character, the inkling through random
     types, the solidification;
The butcher in the slaughter-house, the hands aboard
     schooners and sloops, the raftsman, the pioneer,
Lumbermen in their winter camp, daybreak in the woods,
     stripes of snow on the limbs of trees, the occasional
     snapping,
The glad clear sound of one's own voice, the merry song,
     the natural life of the woods, the strong day's work,
The blazing fire at night, the sweet taste of supper, the talk,
     the bed of hemlock-boughs and the bear-skin;
The house-builder at work in cities or anywhere,
The preparatory jointing, squaring, sawing, mortising,

The hoist-up of beams, the push of them in their places, laying them regular,

Setting the studs by their tenons in the mortises according as they were prepared,

The blows of mallets and hammers, the attitudes of the men, their curv'd limbs,

Bending, standing, astride the beams, driving in pins, holding on by posts and braces,

The hook'd arm over the plate, the other arm wielding the axe,

The floor-men forcing the planks close to be nail'd,

Their postures bringing their weapons downward on the bearers,

The echoes resounding through the vacant building;

The huge storehouse carried up in the city well under way,

The six framing-men, two in the middle and two at each end, carefully bearing on their shoulders a heavy stick for a cross-beam,

The crowded line of masons with trowels in their right hands rapidly laying the long side-wall, two hundred feet from front to rear,

The flexible rise and fall of backs, the continual click of the trowels striking the bricks,

The bricks one after another each laid so workmanlike in its place, and set with a knock of the trowel-handle,

The piles of materials, the mortar on the mortar-boards, and the steady replenishing by the hod-men;

Spar-makers in the spar-yard, the swarming row of well-grown apprentices,

The swing of their axes on the square-hew'd log shaping it
toward the shape of a mast,
The brisk short crackle of the steel driven slantingly into
the pine,
The butter-color'd chips flying off in great flakes and slivers,
The limber motion of brawny young arms and hips in easy
costumes,
The constructor of wharves, bridges, piers, bulk-heads,
floats, stays against the sea;
The city fireman, the fire that suddenly bursts forth in the
close-pack'd square,
The arriving engines, the hoarse shouts, the nimble stepping
and daring,
The strong command through the fire-trumpets, the falling
in line, the rise and fall of the arms forcing the
water,
The slender, spasmic, blue-white jets, the bringing to bear
of the hooks and ladders and their execution,
The crash and cut away of connecting wood-work, or
through floors if the fire smoulders under them,
The crowd with their lit faces watching, the glare and dense
shadows;
The forger at his forge-furnace and the user of iron after
him,
The maker of the axe large and small, and the welder and
temperer,
The chooser breathing his breath on the cold steel and trying
the edge with his thumb,
The one who clean-shapes the handle and sets it firmly in
the socket;

The shadowy processions of the portraits of the past users also,
The primal patient mechanics, the architects and engineers,
The far-off Assyrian edifice and Mizra edifice,
The Roman lictors preceding the consuls,
The antique European warrior with his axe in combat,
The uplifted arm, the clatter of blows on the helmeted head,
The death-howl, the limpsy tumbling body, the rush of friend and foe thither,
The siege of revolted lieges determin'd for liberty,
The summons to surrender, the battering at castle gates, the truce and parley,
The sack of an old city in its time,
The bursting in of mercenaries and bigots tumultuously and disorderly,
Roar, flames, blood, drunkenness, madness,
Goods freely rifled from houses and temples, screams of women in the gripe of brigands,
Craft and thievery of camp-followers, men running, old persons despairing,
The hell of war, the cruelties of creeds,
The list of all executive deeds and words just or unjust,
The power of personality just or unjust.


4

Muscle and pluck forever!
What invigorates life invigorates death,
And the dead advance as much as the living advance,

And the future is no more uncertain than the present,
For the roughness of the earth and of man encloses as much
        as the delicatesse of the earth and of man,
And nothing endures but personal qualities.


What do you think endures?
Do you think a great city endures?
Or a teeming manufacturing state? or a prepared constitu-
        tion? or the best built steamships?
Or hotels of granite and iron? or any chef-d'œuvres of engi-
        neering, forts, armaments?


Away! these are not to be cherish'd for themselves,
They fill their hour, the dancers dance, the musicians play
        for them,
The show passes, all does well enough of course,
All does very well till one flash of defiance.


A great city is that which has the greatest men and women,
If it be a few ragged huts it is still the greatest city in the
        whole world.


5


The place where a great city stands is not the place of
        stretch'd wharves, docks, manufactures, deposits of
        produce merely,
Nor the place of ceaseless salutes of new-comers or the
        anchor-lifters of the departing,

Nor the place of the tallest and costliest buildings or shops selling goods from the rest of the earth,

Nor the place of the best libraries and schools, nor the place where money is plentiest,

Nor the place of the most numerous population.


Where the city stands with the brawniest breed of orators and bards,

Where the city stands that is belov'd by these, and loves them in return and understands them,

Where no monuments exist to heroes but in the common words and deeds,

Where thrift is in its place, and prudence is in its place,

Where the men and women think lightly of the laws,

Where the slave ceases, and the master of slaves ceases,

Where the populace rise at once against the never-ending audacity of elected persons,

Where fierce men and women pour forth as the sea to the whistle of death pours its sweeping and unript waves,

Where outside authority enters always after the precedence of inside authority,

Where the citizen is always the head and ideal, and President, Mayor, Governor and what not, are agents for pay,

Where children are taught to be laws to themselves, and to depend on themselves,

Where equanimity is illustrated in affairs,

Where speculations on the soul are encouraged,

Where women walk in public processions in the streets the
  same as the men,
Where they enter the public assembly and take places the
  same as the men;
Where the city of the faithfulest friends stands,
Where the city of the cleanliness of the sexes stands,
Where the city of the healthiest fathers stands,
Where the city of the best-bodied mothers stands,
There the great city stands.

6

How beggarly appear arguments before a defiant deed!
How the floridness of the materials of cities shrivels before
  a man's or woman's look!

All waits or goes by default till a strong being appears;
A strong being is the proof of the race and of the ability of
  the universe,
When he or she appears materials are overaw'd,
The dispute on the soul stops,
The old customs and phrases are confronted, turn'd back,
  or laid away.

What is your money-making now? what can it do now?
What is your respectability now?
What are your theology, tuition, society, traditions, statute-
  books, now?

Where are your jibes of being now?
Where are your cavils about the soul now?


7

A sterile landscape covers the ore, there is as good as the
        best for all the forbidding appearance,
There is the mine, there are the miners,
The forge-furnace is there, the melt is accomplish'd, the
        hammers-men are at hand with their tongs and ham-
        mers,
What always served and always serves is at hand.
Than this nothing has better served, it has served all,
Served the fluent-tongued and subtle-sensed Greek, and
        long ere the Greek,
Served in building the buildings that last longer than any,
Served the Hebrew, the Persian, the most ancient Hindu-
        stanee,
Served the mound-raiser on the Mississippi, served those
        whose relics remain in Central America,
Served Albic temples in woods or on plains, with unhewn
        pillars and the druids,
Served the artificial clefts, vast, high, silent, on the snow-
        cover'd hills of Scandinavia,
Served those who time out of mind made on the granite
        walls rough sketches of the sun, moon, stars, ships,
        ocean waves,
Served the paths of the irruptions of the Goths, served the
        pastoral tribes and nomads,

Served the long distant Kelt, served the hardy pirates of the
        Baltic,
Served before any of those the venerable and harmless men
        of Ethiopia,
Served the making of helms for the galleys of pleasure and
        the making of those for war,
Served all great works on land and all great works on the
        sea,
For the mediæval ages and before the mediæval ages,
Served not the living only then as now, but served the dead.


8

I see the European headsman,
He stands mask'd, clothed in red, with huge legs and strong
        naked arms,
And leans on a ponderous axe.

(Whom have you slaughter'd lately European headsman?
Whose is that blood upon you so wet and sticky?)

I see the clear sunsets of the martyrs,
I see from the scaffolds the descending ghosts,
Ghosts of dead lords, uncrown'd ladies, impeach'd min-
        isters, rejected kings,
Rivals, traitors, poisoners, disgraced chieftains and the rest.

I see those who in any land have died for the good cause,
The seed is spare, nevertheless the crop shall never run out,

(Mind you O foreign kings, O priests, the crop shall never
    run out.)


I see the blood wash'd entirely away from the axe,
Both blade and helve are clean,
They spirt no more the blood of European nobles, they
    clasp no more the necks of queens.


I see the headsman withdraw and become useless,
I see the scaffold untrodden and mouldy, I see no longer
    any axe upon it,
I see the mighty and friendly emblem of the power of my
    own race, the newest, largest race.


9

(America! I do not vaunt my love for you,
I have what I have.)


The axe leaps!
The solid forest gives fluid utterances,
They tumble forth, they rise and form,
Hut, tent, landing, survey,
Flail, plough, pick, crowbar, spade,
Shingle, rail, prop, wainscot, jamb, lath, panel, gable,
Citadel, ceiling, saloon, academy, organ, exhibition-house,
    library,
Cornice, trellis, pilaster, balcony, window, turret, porch,

Hoe, rake, pitchfork, pencil, wagon, staff, saw, jack-plane,
    mallet, wedge, rounce,
Chair, tub, hoop, table, wicket, vane, sash, floor,
Work-box, chest, string'd instrument, boat, frame, and
    what not,
Capitols of States, and capitols of the nation of States,
Long stately rows in avenues, hospitals for orphans or for
    the poor or sick,
Manhattan steamboats and clippers taking the measure of
    all seas.

The shapes arise!
Shapes of the using of axes anyhow, and the users and all
    that neighbors them,
Cutters down of wood and haulers of it to the Penobscot or
    Kennebec,
Dwellers in cabins among the California mountains or by
    the little lakes, or on the Columbia,
Dwellers south on the banks of the Gila or Rio Grande,
    friendly gatherings, the characters and fun,
Dwellers along the St. Lawrence, or north in Kanada, or
    down by the Yellowstone, dwellers on coasts and
    off coasts,
Seal-fishers, whalers, arctic seamen breaking passages
    through the ice.

The shapes arise!
Shapes of factories, arsenals, foundries, markets,
Shapes of the two-threaded tracks of railroads,

Shapes of the sleepers of bridges, vast frameworks, girders,
       arches,

Shapes of the fleets of barges, tows, lake and canal craft,
       river craft,

Ship-yards and dry-docks along the Eastern and Western
       seas, and in many a bay and by-place,

The live-oak kelsons, the pine planks, the spars, the hack-
       matackroots for knees,

The ships themselves on their ways, the tiers of scaffolds,
       the workmen busy outside and inside,

The tools lying around, the great auger and little auger,
       the adze, bolt line, square, gouge, and bead-plane.


## 10

The shapes arise!

The shape measur'd, saw'd, jack'd, join'd, stain'd,

The coffin-shape for the dead to lie within in his shroud,

The shape got out in posts, in the bedstead posts, in the
       posts of the bride's bed,

The shape of the little trough, the shape of the rockers
       beneath, the shape of the babe's cradle,

The shape of the floor-planks, the floor-planks for dancers'
       feet,

The shape of the planks of the family home, the home of
       the friendly parents and children,

The shape of the roof of the home of the happy young man
       and woman, the roof over the well-married young
       man and woman,

The roof over the supper joyously cook'd by the chaste wife,
and joyously eaten by the chaste husband, content
after his day's work.


The shapes arise!
The shape of the prisoner's place in the court-room, and of
him or her seated in the place,
The shape of the liquor-bar lean'd against by the young
rum-drinker and the old rum-drinker,
The shape of the shamed and angry stairs trod by sneaking
footsteps,
The shape of the sly settee, and the adulterous unwhole-
some couple,
The shape of the gambling-board with its devilish winnings
and losings,
The shape of the step-ladder for the convicted and sentenced
murderer, the murderer with haggard face and
pinion'd arms,
The sheriff at hand with his deputies, the silent and white-
lipp'd crowd, the dangling of the rope.


The shapes arise!
Shapes of doors giving many exits and entrances,
The door passing the dissever'd friend flush'd and in haste,
The door that admits good news and bad news,
The door whence the son left home confident and puff'd up,
The door he enter'd again from a long and scandalous ab-
sence, diseas'd, broken down, without innocence,
without means.

## 11

Her shape arises,

She less guarded than ever, yet more guarded than ever,

The gross and soil'd she moves among do not make her
gross and soil'd,

She knows the thoughts as she passes, nothing is conceal'd
from her,

She is none the less considerate or friendly therefor,

She is the best belov'd, it is without exception, she has no
reason to fear and she does not fear,

Oaths, quarrels, hiccupp'd songs, smutty expressions, are
idle to her as she passes,

She is silent, she is possess'd of herself, they do not offend
her,

She receives them as the laws of Nature receive them, she is
strong,

She too is a law of Nature—there is no law stronger than
she is.


12

The main shapes arise!

Shapes of Democracy total, result of centuries,

Shapes ever projecting other shapes,

Shapes of turbulent manly cities,

Shapes of the friends and home-givers of the whole earth,

Shapes bracing the earth and braced with the whole earth.

# Pioneers! O Pioneers!

Come my tan-faced children,
Follow well in order, get your weapons ready,
Have you your pistols? have you your sharp-edged axes?
    Pioneers! O pioneers!

For we cannot tarry here,
We must march my darlings, we must bear the brunt of
   danger,
We the youthful sinewy races, all the rest on us depend,
    Pioneers! O pioneers!

O you youths, Western youths,
So impatient, full of action, full of manly pride and friend-
   ship,
Plain I see you Western youths, see you tramping with the
   foremost,
    Pioneers! O pioneers!

Have the elder races halted?
Do they droop and end their lesson, wearied over there
   beyond the seas?

We take up the task eternal, and the burden and the lesson,
　　　　Pioneers! O pioneers!


　　　All the past we leave behind,
We debouch upon a newer mightier world, varied world,
Fresh and strong the world we seize, world of labor and the
　　　march,
　　　　Pioneers! O pioneers!


　　　We detachments steady throwing,
Down the edges, through the passes, up the mountains
　　　steep,
Conquering, holding, daring, venturing as we go the un-
　　　known ways,
　　　　Pioneers! O pioneers!


　　　We primeval forests felling,
We the rivers stemming, vexing we and piercing deep the
　　　mines within,
We the surface broad surveying, we the virgin soil up-
　　　heaving,
　　　　Pioneers! O pioneers!


　　　Colorado men are we,
From the peaks gigantic, from the great sierras and the
　　　high plateaus,
From the mine and from the gully, from the hunting trail
　　　we come,
　　　　Pioneers! O pioneers!

From Nebraska, from Arkansas,
Central inland race are we, from Missouri, with the con-
tinental blood intervein'd,
All the hands of comrades clasping, all the Southern, all
the Northern,
　　　Pioneers! O pioneers!


　　　O resistless restless race!
O beloved race in all! O my breast aches with tender love
for all!
O I mourn and yet exult, I am rapt with love for all,
　　　Pioneers! O pioneers!


　　　Raise the mighty mother mistress,
Waving high the delicate mistress, over all the starry mis-
tress, (bend your heads all,)
Raise the fang'd and warlike mistress, stern, impassive,
weapon'd mistress,
　　　Pioneers! O pioneers!


　　　See my children, resolute children,
By those swarms upon our rear we must never yield or falter,
Ages back in ghostly millions frowning there behind us
urging,
　　　Pioneers! O pioneers!


　　　On and on the compact ranks,
With accessions ever waiting, with the places of the dead
quickly fill'd,

Through the battle, through defeat, moving yet and never
       stopping,
           Pioneers! O pioneers!


          O to die advancing on!
Are there some of us to droop and die? has the hour come?
Then upon the march we fittest die, soon and sure the gap
       is fill'd,
           Pioneers! O pioneers!


          All the pulses of the world,
Falling in they beat for us, with the Western movement
       beat,
Holding single or together, steady moving to the front, all
       for us,
           Pioneers! O pioneers!


          Life's involv'd and varied pageants,
All the forms and shows, all the workmen at their work,
All the seamen and the landsmen, all the masters with their
       slaves,
           Pioneers! O pioneers!


          All the hapless silent lovers,
All the prisoners in the prisons, all the righteous and the
       wicked,
All the joyous, all the sorrowing, all the living, all the
       dying,
           Pioneers! O pioneers!

I too with my soul and body,
We, a curious trio, picking, wandering on our way,
Through these shores amid the shadows, with the appari-
tions pressing,
Pioneers! O pioneers!


Lo, the darting bowling orb!
Lo, the brother orbs around, all the clustering suns and
planets,
All the dazzling days, all the mystic nights with dreams,
Pioneers! O pioneers!


These are of us, they are with us,
All for primal needed work, while the followers there in
embryo wait behind,
We to-day's procession heading, we the route for travel
clearing,
Pioneers! O pioneers!


O you daughters of the West!
O you young and elder daughters! O you mothers and you
wives!
Never must you be divided, in our ranks you move united,
Pioneers! O pioneers!


Minstrels latent on the prairies!
(Shrouded bards of other lands, you may rest, you have
done your work,)

Soon I hear you coming warbling, soon you rise and tramp
amid us,
Pioneers! O pioneers!


Not for delectations sweet,
Not the cushion and the slipper, not the peaceful and the
studious,
Not the riches safe and palling, not for us the tame enjoy-
ment,
Pioneers! O pioneers!


Do the feasters gluttonous feast?
Do the corpulent sleepers sleep? have they lock'd and bolted
doors?
Still be ours the diet hard, and the blanket on the ground,
Pioneers! O pioneers!


Has the night descended?
Was the road of late so toilsome? did we stop discouraged
nodding on our way?
Yet a passing hour I yield you in your tracks to pause ob-
livious,
Pioneers! O pioneers!


Till with sound of trumpet,
Far, far off the daybreak call—hark! how loud and clear I
hear it wind,
Swift! to the head of the army!—swift! spring to your
places,
Pioneers! O pioneers!

# Year of Meteors

(*1859-60*)

Year of meteors! brooding year!
I would bind in words retrospective some of your deeds and
  signs,
I would sing your contest for the 19th Presidentiad,
I would sing how an old man, tall, with white hair, mounted
  the scaffold in Virginia,
(I was at hand, silent I stood with teeth shut close, I watch'd,
I stood very near you old man when cool and indifferent,
  but trembling with age and your unheal'd wounds
  you mounted the scaffold;)
I would sing in my copious song your census returns of the
  States,
The tables of population and products, I would sing of your
  ships and their cargoes,
The proud black ships of Manhattan arriving, some fill'd
  with immigrants, some from the isthmus with
  cargoes of gold,
Songs thereof would I sing, to all that hitherward comes
  would I welcome give,
And you would I sing fair stripling! welcome to you from
  me, young prince of England!

(Remember you surging Manhattan's crowds as you pass'd
with your cortege of nobles?
There in the crowds stood I, and singled you out with at-
tachment;)
Nor forget I to sing of the wonder, the ship as she swam up
my bay,
Well-shaped and stately the Great Eastern swamp up my
bay, she was 600 feet long,
Her moving swiftly surrounded by myriads of small craft
I forget not to sing;
Nor the comet that came unannounced out of the north flar-
ing in heaven,
Nor the strange huge meteor-procession dazzling and clear
shooting over our heads,
(A moment, a moment long it sail'd its balls of unearthly
light over our heads,
Then departed, dropt in the night, and was gone;)
Of such, and fitful as they, I sing—with gleams from them
would I gleam and patch these chants,
Your chants, O year all mottled with evil and good—year
of forebodings!
Year of comets and meteors transient and strange—lo! even
here one equally transient and strange!
As I flit through you hastily, soon to fall and be gone, what
is this chant,
What am I myself but one of your meteors?

# A Broadway Pageant

Over the Western sea hither from Niphon come,
Courteous, the swart-cheek'd two-sworded envoys,
Leaning back in their open barouches, bare-headed, im-
      passive,
Ride to-day through Manhattan.

Libertad! I do not know whether others behold what I
      behold,
In the procession along with the nobles of Niphon, the
      errand-bearers,
Bringing up the rear, hovering above, around, or in the
      ranks marching,
But I will sing you a song of what I behold Libertad.

When million-footed Manhattan unpent descends to her
      pavements,
When the thunder-cracking guns arouse me with the proud
      roar I love,
When the round-mouth'd guns out of the smoke and smell
      I love spit their salutes,

When the fire-flashing guns have fully alerted me, and
    heaven-clouds canopy my city with a delicate thin
    haze,
When gorgeous the countless straight stems, the forests at
    the wharves, thicken with colors,
When every ship richly drest carries her flag at the peak,
When pennants trail and street-festoons hang from the
    windows,
When Broadway is entirely given up to foot-passengers and
    foot-standers, when the mass is densest,
When the façades of the houses are alive with people, when
    eyes gaze riveted tens of thousands at a time,
When the guests from the islands advance, when the
    pageant moves forward visible,
When the summons is made, when the answer that waited
    thousands of years answers,
I too arising, answering, descend to the pavements, merge
    with the crowd, and gaze with them.


2


Superb-faced Manhattan!
Comrade Americanos! to us, then at last the Orient comes.


To us, my city,
Where our tall-topt marble and iron beauties range on op-
    posite sides, to walk in the space between,
To-day our Antipodes comes.

The Originatress comes,
The nest of languages, the bequeather of poems, the race
of eld,
Florid with blood, pensive, rapt with musings, hot with
passion,
Sultry with perfume, with ample and flowing garments,
With sunburnt visage, with intense soul and glittering eyes,
The race of Brahma comes.

See my cantabile! these and more are flashing to us from the
procession,
As it moves changing, a kaleidoscope divine it moves chang-
ing before us.

For not the envoys nor the tann'd Japanee from his island
only,
Lithe and silent the Hindoo appears, the Asiatic continent
itself appears, the past, the dead,
The murky night-morning of wonder and fable inscrutable,
The envelop'd mysteries, the old and unknown hive-bees,
The north, the sweltering south, eastern Assyria, the He-
brews, the ancient of ancients,
Vast desolated cities, the gliding present, all of these and
more are in the pageant-procession.

Geography, the world, is in it,
The Great Sea, the brood of islands, Polynesia, the coast
beyond,
The coast you henceforth are facing—you Libertad! from
your Western golden shores,

The countries there with their populations, the millions en-
masse are curiously here,
The swarming market-places, the temples with idols ranged
along the sides or at the end, bonze, brahmin, and
llama,
Mandarin, farmer, merchant, mechanic, and fisherman,
The singing-girl and the dancing-girl, the ecstatic persons,
the secluded emperors,
Confucius himself, the great poets and heroes, the warriors,
the castes, all,
Trooping up, crowding from all directions, from the Altay
mountains,
From Thibet, from the four winding and far-flowing rivers
of China,
From the southern peninsulas and the demi-continental
islands, from Malaysia,
These and whatever belongs to them palpable show forth
to me, and are seiz'd by me,
And I am seiz'd by them, and friendlily held by them,
Till as here them all I chant, Libertad! for themselves and
for you.


For I too raising my voice join the ranks of this pageant,
I am the chanter, I chant aloud over the pageant,
I chant the world on my Western sea,
I chant copious the islands beyond, thick as stars in the sky,
I chant the new empire grander than any before, as in a
vision it comes to me,
I chant America the mistress, I chant a greater supremacy,

I chant projected a thousand blooming cities yet in time on
        those groups of sea-islands,
My sail-ships and steam-ships threading the archipelagoes,
My stars and stripes fluttering in the wind,
Commerce opening, the sleep of ages having done its work,
        races reborn, refresh'd,
Lives, works resumed—the object I know not—but the old,
        the Asiatic renew'd as it must be,
Commencing from this day surrounded by the world.


### 3

And you Libertad of the world!
You shall sit in the middle well-pois'd thousands and thou-
        sands of years,
As to-day from one side the nobles of Asia come to you,
As to-morrow from the other side the queen of England
        sends her eldest son to you.
The sign is reversing, the orb is enclosed,
The ring is circled, the journey is done,
The box-lid is but perceptibly open'd, nevertheless the per-
        fume pours copiously out of the whole box.


Young Libertad! with the venerable Asia, the all-mother,
Be considerate with her now and ever hot Libertad, for you
        are all,
Bend your proud neck to the long-off mother now sending
        messages over the archipelagoes to you,
Bend your proud neck low for once, young Libertad.

Were the children straying westward so long? so wide the
      tramping?
Were the precedent dim ages debouching westward from
      Paradise so long?
Were the centuries steadily footing it that way, all the
      while unknown, for you, for reasons?

They are justified, they are accomplish'd, they shall now
      be turn'd the other way also, to travel toward you
      thence,
They shall now also march obediently eastward for your
      sake Libertad.

# Sea-Drift

## OUT OF THE CRADLE ENDLESSLY ROCKING

Out of the cradle endlessly rocking,
Out of the mocking-bird's throat, the musical shuttle,
Out of the Ninth-month midnight,
Over the sterile sands and the fields beyond, where the
       child leaving his bed wander'd alone, bareheaded,
       barefoot,
Down from the shower'd halo,
Up from the mystic play of shadows twining and twisting
       as if they were alive,
Out from the patches of briers and blackberries,
From the memories of the bird that chanted to me,
From your memories sad brother, from the fitful risings and
       fallings I heard,
From under that yellow half-moon late-risen and swollen
       as if with tears,
From those beginning notes of yearning and love there in
       the mist,
From the thousand responses of my heart never to cease,
From the myriad thence-arous'd words,

From the word stronger and more delicious than any,
From such as now they start the scene revisiting,
As a flock, twittering, rising, or overhead passing,
Borne hither, ere all eludes me, hurriedly,
A man, yet by these tears a little boy again,
Throwing myself on the sand, confronting the waves,
I, chanter of pains and joys, uniter of here and hereafter,
Taking all hints to use them, but swiftly leaping beyond
       them,
A reminiscence sing.


Once Paumanok,
When the lilac-scent was in the air and Fifth-month grass
       was growing,
Up this seashore in some briers,
Two feather'd guests from Alabama, two together,
And their nest, and four light-green eggs spotted with
       brown,
And every day the he-bird to and fro near at hand,
And every day the she-bird crouch'd on her nest, silent, with
       bright eyes,
And every day I, a curious boy, never too close, never dis-
       turbing them,
Cautiously peering, absorbing, translating.


*Shine! shine! shine!*
*Pour down your warmth, great sun!*
*While we bask, we two together.*

*Two together!*
*Winds blow south, or winds blow north,*
*Day come white, or night come black,*
*Home, or rivers and mountains from home,*
*Singing all time, minding no time,*
*While we two keep together.*


Till of a sudden,
May-be kill'd unknown to her mate,
One forenoon the she-bird crouch'd not on the nest,
Nor return'd that afternoon, nor the next,
Nor ever appear'd again.


And thenceforward all summer in the sound of the sea,
And at night under the full of the moon in calmer weather,
Over the hoarse surging of the sea,
Or flitting from brier to brier by day,
I saw, I heard at intervals the remaining one, the he-bird,
The solitary guest from Alabama.


*Blow! blow! blow!*
*Blow up sea-winds along Paumanok's shore;*
*I wait and I wait till you blow my mate to me.*


Yes, when the stars glisten'd,
All night long on the prong of a moss-scallop'd stake,
Down almost amid the slapping waves,
Sat the lone singer wonderful causing tears.

He call'd on his mate,
He pour'd forth the meanings which I of all men know.


Yes my brother I know,
The rest might not, but I have treasur'd every note,
For more than once dimly down to the beach gliding,
Silent, avoiding the moonbeams, blending myself with the
        shadows,
Recalling now the obscure shapes, the echoes, the sounds
        and sights after their sorts,
The white arms out in the breakers tirelessly tossing,
I, with bare feet, a child, the wind wafting my hair,
Listen'd long and long.


Listen'd to keep, to sing, now translating the notes,
Following you my brother.


*Soothe! soothe! soothe!*
*Close on its wave soothes the wave behind,*
*And again another behind embracing and lapping, every*
        *one close,*
*But my love soothes not me, not me.*


*Low hangs the moon, it rose late,*
*It is lagging—O I think it is heavy with love, with love.*


*O madly the sea pushes upon the land,*
*With love, with love.*

*O night! do I not see my love fluttering out among the*
        *breakers?*
*What is that little black thing I see there in the white?*

*Loud! loud! loud!*
*Loud I call to you, my love!*

*High and clear I shoot my voice over the waves,*
*Surely you must know who is here, is here,*
*You must know who I am, my love.*

*Low-hanging moon!*
*What is that dusky spot in your brown yellow?*
*O it is the shape, the shape of my mate!*
*O moon do not keep her from me any longer.*

*Land! land! O land!*
*Whichever way I turn, O I think you could give me my mate*
        *back again if you only would,*
*For I am almost sure I see her dimly whichever way I look.*

*O rising stars!*
*Perhaps the one I want so much will rise, will rise with some*
        *of you.*

*O throat! O trembling throat!*
*Sound clearer through the atmosphere!*
*Pierce the woods, the earth,*
*Somewhere listening to catch you must be the one I want.*

*Shake out carols!*
*Solitary here, the night's carols!*
*Carols of lonesome love! death's carols!*
*Carols under that lagging, yellow, waning moon!*
*O under that moon where she droops almost down into the*
        *sea!*
*O reckless despairing carols.*

*But soft! sink low!*
*Soft! let me just murmur,*
*And do you wait a moment you husky-nois'd sea,*
*For somewhere I believe I heard my mate responding to me,*
*So faint, I must be still, be still to listen,*
*But not altogether still, for then she might not come im-*
        *mediately to me.*

*Hither my love!*
*Here I am! here!*
*With this just-sustain'd note I announce myself to you,*
*This gentle call is for you my love, for you.*

*Do not be decoy'd elsewhere,*
*That is the whistle of the wind, it is not my voice,*
*That is the fluttering, the fluttering of the spray,*
*Those are the shadows of leaves.*

*O darkness! O in vain!*
*O I am very sick and sorrowful.*

*O brown halo in the sky near the moon, drooping upon the*
      *sea!*
*O troubled reflection in the sea!*
*O throat! O throbbing heart!*
*And I singing uselessly, uselessly all the night.*

*O past! O happy life! O songs of joy!*
*In the air, in the woods, over fields,*
*Loved! loved! loved! loved! loved!*
*But my mate no more, no more with me!*
*We two together no more.*

The aria sinking,
All else continuing, the stars shining,
The winds blowing, the notes of the bird continuous
      echoing,
With angry moans the fierce old mother incessantly
      moaning,
On the sands of Paumanok's shore gray and rustling,
The yellow half-moon enlarged, sagging down, drooping,
      the face of the sea almost touching,
The boy ecstatic, with his bare feet the waves, with his hair
      the atmosphere dallying,
The love in the heart long pent, now loose, now at last
      tumultuously bursting,
The aria's meaning, the ears, the soul, swiftly depositing,
The strange tears down the cheeks coursing,
The colloquy there, the trio, each uttering,
The undertone, the savage old mother incessantly crying,

To the boy's soul's questions sullenly timing, some drown'd
        secret hissing,
To the outsetting bard.


Demon or bird (said the boy's soul,)
Is it indeed toward your mate you sing? or is it really to me?
For I, that was a child, my tongue's use sleeping, now I
        have heard you,
Now in a moment I know what I am for, I awake,
And already a thousand singers, a thousand songs, clearer,
        louder and more sorrowful than yours,
A thousand warbling echoes have started to life within me,
        never to die.


O you singer solitary, singing by yourself, projecting me,
O solitary me listening, never more shall I cease perpetuat-
        ing you,
Never more shall I escape, never more the reverberations,
Never more the cries of unsatisfied love be absent from me,
Never again leave me to be the peaceful child I was before,
        what there in the night,
By the sea under the yellow and sagging moon,
The messenger there arous'd, the fire, the sweet hell within,
The unknown want, the destiny of me.


O give me the clew! (it lurks in the night here somewhere,)
O if I am to have so much, let me have more!


A word then, (for I will conquer it,)
The word final, superior to all,

Subtle, sent up—what is it?—I listen;
Are you whispering it, and have been all the time, you sea-
      waves?
Is that it from your liquid rims and wet sands?

Whereto answering, the sea,
Delaying not, hurrying not,
Whisper'd me through the night, and very plainly before
      daybreak,
Lisp'd to me the low and delicious word death,
And again death, death, death, death,
Hissing melodious, neither like the bird nor like my arous'd
      child's heart,
But edging near as privately for me rustling at my feet,
Creeping thence steadily up to my ears and laving me softly
      all over,
Death, death, death, death, death.

Which I do not forget,
But fuse the song of my dusky demon and brother,
That he sang to me in the moonlight on Paumanok's gray
      beach,
With the thousand responsive songs at random,
My own songs awaked from that hour,
And with them the key, the word up from the waves,
The word of the sweetest song and all songs,
That strong and delicious word which, creeping to my feet,
(Or like some old crone rocking the cradle, swathed in
      sweet garments, bending aside,)
The sea whisper'd me.

# AS I EBB'D WITH THE OCEAN OF LIFE

1

As I ebb'd with the ocean of life,
As I wended the shores I know,
As I walk'd where the ripples continually wash you
    Paumanok,
Where they rustle up hoarse and sibilant,
Where the fierce old mother endlessly cries for her cast-
    aways,
I musing late in the autumn day, gazing off southward,
Held by this electric self out of the pride of which I utter
    poems,
Was seiz'd by the spirit that trails in the lines underfoot,
The rim, the sediment that stands for all the water and all
    the land of the globe.


Fascinated, my eyes reverting from the south, dropt, to
    follow those slender windrows,
Chaff, straw, splinters of wood, weeds, and the sea-gluten,
Scum, scales from shining rocks, leaves of salt-lettuce, left
    by the tide,
Miles walking, the sound of breaking waves the other side
    of me,
Paumanok there and then as I thought the old thought of
    likenesses,
These you presented to me you fish-shaped island,
As I wended the shores I know,
As I walk'd with that electric self seeking types.

As I wend to the shores I know not,
As I list to the dirge, the voices of men and women wreck'd,
As I inhale the impalpable breezes that set in upon me,
As the ocean so mysterious rolls toward me closer and closer,
I too but signify at the utmost a little wash'd-up drift,
A few sands and dead leaves to gather,
Gather, and merge myself as part of the sands and drift.


O baffled, balk'd, bent to the very earth,
Oppress'd with myself that I have dared to open my mouth,
Aware now that amid all that blab whose echoes recoil upon
      me I have not once had the least idea who or what
      I am,
But that before all my arrogant poems the real Me stands yet
      untouch'd, untold, altogether unreach'd,
Withdrawn far, mocking me with mock-congratulatory
      signs and bows,
With peals of distant ironical laughter at every word I have
      written,
Pointing in silence to these songs, and then to the sand
      beneath,
I perceive I have not really understood any thing, not a
      single object, and that no man ever can,
Nature here in sight of the sea taking advantage of me to
      dart upon me and sting me,
Because I have dared to open my mouth to sing at all.

## 3

You oceans both, I close with you,
We murmur alike reproachfully rolling sands and drift,
      knowing not why,
These little shreds indeed standing for you and me and all.

You friable shore with trails of debris,
You fish-shaped island, I take what is underfoot,
What is yours is mine my father.

I too Paumanok,
I too have bubbled up, floated the measureless float, and
      been wash'd on your shores,
I too am but a trail of drift and debris,
I too leave little wrecks upon you, you fish-shaped island.

I throw myself upon your breast my father,
I cling to you so that you cannot unloose me,
I hold you so firm till you answer me something.

Kiss me my father,
Touch me with your lips as I touch those I love,
Breathe to me while I hold you close the secret of the mur-
      muring I envy.

## 4

Ebb, ocean of life, (the flow will return,)
Cease not your moaning you fierce old mother,

Endlessly cry for your castaways, but fear not, deny not me,
Rustle not up so hoarse and angry against my feet as I touch
you or gather from you.


I mean tenderly by you and all,
I gather for myself and for this phantom looking down
where we lead, and following me and mine.


Me and mine, loose windrows, little corpses
Froth, snowy white, and bubbles,
(See, from my dead lips the ooze exuding at last,
See, the prismatic colors glistening and rolling,)
Tufts of straw, sands, fragments,
Buoy'd hither from many moods, one contradicting another,
From the storm, the long calm, the darkness, the swell,
Musing, pondering, a breath, a briny tear, a dab of liquid
or soil,
Up just as much out of fathomless workings fermented and
thrown,
A limp blossom or two, torn, just as much over waves float-
ing, drifted at random,
Just as much for us that sobbing dirge of Nature,
Just as much whence we come that blare of the cloud-
trumpets,
We, capricious, brought hither we know not whence, spread
out before you,
You up there walking or sitting,
Whoever you are, we too lie in drifts at your feet.

217

# TEARS

Tears! tears! tears!
In the night, in solitude, tears,
On the white shore dripping, dripping, suck'd in by the
sand,
Tears, not a star shining, all dark and desolate,
Moist tears from the eyes of a muffled head;
O who is that ghost? that form in the dark, with tears?
What shapeless lump is that, bent, crouch'd there on the
sand?
Streaming tears, sobbing tears, throes, choked with wild
cries;
O storm, embodied, rising, careering with swift steps along
the beach!
O wild and dismal night storm, with wind—O belching and
desperate!
O shade so sedate and decorous by day, with calm counte-
nance and regulated pace,
But away at night as you fly, none looking—O then the un-
loosen'd ocean,
Of tears! tears! tears!


# ON THE BEACH AT NIGHT

On the beach at night,
Stands a child with her father,
Watching the east, the autumn sky.

Up through the darkness,
While ravening clouds, the burial clouds, in black masses
      spreading,
Lower sullen and fast athwart and down the sky,
Amid a transparent clear belt of ether yet left in the east,
Ascends large and calm the lord-star Jupiter,
And nigh at hand, only a very little above,
Swim the delicate sisters the Pleiades.


From the beach the child holding the hand of her father,
Those burial-clouds that lower victorious soon to devour
      all,
Watching, silently weeps.


Weep not, child,
Weep not, my darling,
With these kisses let me remove your tears,
The ravening clouds shall not long be victorious,
They shall not long possess the sky, they devour the stars
      only in apparition,
Jupiter shall emerge, be patient, watch again another night,
      the Pleiades shall emerge,
They are immortal, all those stars both silvery and golden
      shall shine out again,
The great stars and the little ones shall shine out again, they
      endure,
The vast immortal suns and the long-enduring pensive
      moons shall again shine.

Then dearest child mournest thou only for Jupiter?
Considerest thou alone the burial of the stars?

Something there is,
(With my lips soothing thee, adding I whisper,
I give thee the first suggestion, the problem and indirec-
        tion,)
Something there is more immortal even than the stars,
(Many the burials, many the days and nights, passing
        away,)
Something that shall endure longer even than lustrous
        Jupiter,
Longer than sun or any revolving satellite,
Or the radiant sisters the Pleiades.

## THE WORLD BELOW THE BRINE

The world below the brine,
Forests at the bottom of the sea, the branches and leaves,
Sea-lettuce, vast lichens, strange flowers and seeds, the
        thick tangle, openings, and pink turf,
Different colors, pale gray and green, purple, white, and
        gold, the play of light through the water,
Dumb swimmers there among the rocks, coral, gluten,
        grass, rushes, and the aliment of the swimmers,
Sluggish existences grazing there suspended, or slowly
        crawling close to the bottom,

The sperm-whale at the surface blowing air and spray, or
       disporting with his flukes,
The leaden-eyed shark, the walrus, the turtle, the hairy sea-
       leopard, and the sting-ray,
Passions there, wars, pursuits, tribes, sight in those ocean-
       depths, breathing that thick-breathing air, as so
       many do,
The change thence to the sight here, and to the subtle air
       breathed by beings like us who walk this sphere,
The change onward from ours to that of beings who walk
       other spheres.


## ON THE BEACH AT NIGHT ALONE

On the beach at night alone,
As the old mother sways her to and fro singing her husky
       song,
As I watch the bright stars shining, I think a thought of the
       clef of the universes and of the future.


A vast similitude interlocks all,
All spheres, grown, ungrown, small, large, suns, moons,
       planets,
All distances of place however wide,
All distances of time, all inanimate forms,
All souls, all living bodies though they be ever so different,
       or in different worlds,

All gaseous, watery, vegetable, mineral processes, the fishes,
    the brutes,
All nations, colors, barbarisms, civilizations, languages,
All identities that have existed or may exist on this globe,
    or any globe,
All lives and deaths, all of the past, present, future,
This vast similitude spans them, and always has spann'd,
And shall forever span them and compactly hold and enclose
    them.


## SONG FOR ALL SEAS, ALL SHIPS

### I

To-day a rude brief recitative,
Of ships sailing the seas, each with its special flag or ship-
    signal,
Of unnamed heroes in the ships—of waves spreading and
    spreading far as the eye can reach,
Of dashing spray, and the winds piping and blowing,
And out of these a chant for the sailors of all nations,
Fitful, like a surge.

Of sea-captains young or old, and the mates, and of all
    intrepid sailors,
Of the few, very choice, taciturn, whom fate can never
    surprise nor death dismay,
Pick'd sparingly without noise by thee old ocean, chosen
    by thee,

Thou sea that pickest and cullest the race in time, and
    unitest nations,
Suckled by thee, old husky nurse, embodying thee,
Indomitable, untamed as thee.


(Ever the heroes on water or on land, by one or twos
    appearing,
Ever the stock preserv'd and never lost, though rare, enough
    for seed preserv'd.)


### 2

Flaunt out O sea your separate flags of nations!
Flaunt out visible as ever the various ship-signals!
But do you reserve especially for yourself and for the soul
    of man one flag above all the rest,
A spiritual woven signal for all nations, emblem of man
    elate above death,
Token of all brave captains and all intrepid sailors and
    mates,
And all that went down doing their duty,
Reminiscent of them, twined from all intrepid captains
    young or old,
A pennant universal, subtly waving all time, o'er all brave
    sailors,
All seas, all ships.

# PATROLING BARNEGAT

Wild, wild the storm, and the sea high running,
Steady the roar of the gale, with incessant undertone mutter-
    ing,
Shouts of demoniac laughter fitfully piercing and pealing,
Waves, air, midnight, their savagest trinity lashing,
Out in the shadows there milk-white combs careering,
On beachy slush and sand spirts of snow fierce slanting,
Where through the murk the easterly death-wind breasting,
Through cutting swirl and spray watchful and firm ad-
    vancing,
(That in the distance! is that a wreck? is the red signal
    flaring?)
Slush and sand of the beach tireless till daylight wending,
Steadily, slowly, through hoarse roar never remitting,
Along the midnight edge by those milk-white combs career-
    ing,
A group of dim, weird forms, struggling, the night con-
    fronting,
That savage trinity warily watching.


# AFTER THE SEA-SHIP

After the sea-ship, after the whistling winds,
After the white-gray sails taut to their spars and ropes,
Below, a myriad myriad waves hastening, lifting up their
    necks,

Tending in ceaseless flow toward the track of the ship,
Waves of the ocean bubbling and gurgling, blithely prying,
Waves, undulating waves, liquid, uneven, emulous waves,
Toward that whirling current, laughing and buoyant, with
      curves,
Where the great vessel sailing and tacking displaced the
      surface,
Larger and smaller waves in the spread of the ocean yearn-
      fully flowing,
The wake of the sea-ship after she passes, flashing and
      frolicsome under the sun,
A motley procession with many a fleck of foam and many
      fragments,
Following the stately and rapid ship, in the wake following.


## WHEN I HEARD THE LEARN'D ASTRONOMER

When I heard the learn'd astronomer,
When the proofs, the figures, were ranged in columns
      before me,
When I was shown the charts and diagrams, to add, divide,
      and measure them,
When I sitting heard the astronomer where he lectured
      with much applause in the lecture-room,
How soon unaccountable I became tired and sick,
Till rising and gliding out I wander'd off by myself,
In the mystical moist night-air, and from time to time,
Look'd up in perfect silence at the stars.

# Drum-Taps

## FIRST O SONGS FOR A PRELUDE

First O songs for a prelude,
Lightly strike on the stretch'd tympanum pride and joy in
      my city,
How she led the rest to arms, how she gave the cue,
How at once with lithe limbs unwaiting a moment she
      sprang,
(O superb! O Manhattan, my own, my peerless!
O strongest you in the hour of danger, in crisis! O truer than
      steel!)
How you sprang—how you threw off the costumes of peace
      with indifferent hand,
How your soft opera-music changed, and the drum and fife
      were heard in their stead,
How you led to the war, (that shall serve for our prelude,
      songs of soldiers,)
How Manhattan drum-taps led.

Forty years had I in my city seen soldiers parading,
Forty years as a pageant, till unawares the lady of this
      teeming and turbulent city,

Sleepless amid her ships, her houses, her incalculable
    wealth,
With her million children around her, suddenly,
At dead of night, at news from the south,
Incens'd struck with clinch'd hand the pavement.


A shock electric, the night sustain'd it,
Till with ominous hum our hive at daybreak pour'd out its
    myriads.


From the houses then and the workshops, and through all
    the doorways,
Leapt they tumultuous, and lo! Manhattan arming.


To the drum-taps prompt,
The young men falling in and arming,
The mechanics arming, (the trowel, the jack-plane, the
    blacksmith's hammer, tost aside with precipitation,)
The lawyer leaving his office and arming, the judge leaving
    the court,
The driver deserting his wagon in the street, jumping down,
    throwing the reins abruptly down on the horses'
    backs,
The salesman leaving the store, the boss, book-keeper,
    porter, all leaving;
Squads gather everywhere by common consent and arm,
The new recruits, even boys, the old men show them how to
    wear their accoutrements, they buckle the straps
    carefully,

Outdoors arming, indoors arming, the flash of the musket-
barrels,

The white tents cluster in camps, the arm'd sentries around,
the sunrise cannon and again at sunset,

Arm'd regiments arrive every day, pass through the city,
and embark from the wharves,

(How good they look as they tramp down to the river,
sweaty, with their guns on their shoulders!

How I love them! how I could hug them, with their brown
faces and their clothes and knapsacks cover'd with
dust!)

The blood of the city up—arm'd! arm'd! the cry everywhere,

The flags flung out from the steeples of churches and from
all the public buildings and stores,

The tearful parting, the mother kisses her son, the son kisses
his mother,

(Loth is the mother to part, yet not a word does she speak
to detain him,)

The tumultuous escort, the ranks of policemen preceding,
clearing the way,

The unpent enthusiasm, the wild cheers of the crowd for
their favorites,

The artillery, the silent cannons bright as gold, drawn
along, rumble lightly over the stones,

(Silent cannons, soon to cease your silence,

Soon unlimber'd to begin the red business;)

All the mutter of preparation, all the determin'd arming,

The hospital service, the lint, bandages and medicines,

The women volunteering for nurses, the work begun for
in earnest, no mere parade now;

War! an arm'd race is advancing! the welcome for battle,
     no turning away;
War! be it weeks, months, or years, an arm'd race is advanc-
     ing to welcome it.

Mannahatta a-march—and it's O to sing it well!
It's O for a manly life in the camp.

And the sturdy artillery,
The guns bright as gold, the work for giants, to serve well
     the guns,
Unlimber them! (no more as the past forty years for salutes
     for courtesies merely,
Put in something now besides powder and wadding.)

And you lady of ships, you Mannahatta,
Old matron of this proud, friendly, turbulent city,
Often in peace and wealth you were pensive or covertly
     frown'd amid all your children,
But now you smile with joy exulting old Mannahatta.


## EIGHTEEN SIXTY-ONE

Arm'd year—year of the struggle,
No dainty rhymes or sentimental love verses for you ter-
     rible year,
Not you as some pale poetling seated at a desk lisping
     cadenzas piano,

229

But as a strong man erect, clothed in blue clothes, advanc-
      ing, carrying a rifle on your shoulder,
With well-gristled body and sunburnt face and hands, with
      a knife in the belt at your side,
As I heard you shouting loud, your sonorous voice ringing
      across the continent,
Your masculine voice O year, as rising amid the great cities,
Amid the men of Manhattan I saw you as one of the work-
      men, the dwellers in Manhattan,
Or with large steps crossing the prairies out of Illinois and
      Indiana,
Rapidly crossing the West with springy gait and descending
      the Alleghanies,
Or down from the great lakes or in Pennsylvania, or on
      deck along the Ohio river,
Or southward along the Tennessee or Cumberland rivers, or
      at Chattanooga on the mountain top,
Saw I your gait and saw I your sinewy limbs clothed in
      blue, bearing weapons, robust year,
Heard your determin'd voice launch'd forth again and
      again,
Year that suddenly sang by the mouths of the round-lipp'd
      cannon,
I repeat you, hurrying, crashing, sad, distracted year.

# BEAT! BEAT! DRUMS!

Beat! beat! drums!—blow! bugles! blow!
Through the windows—through doors—burst like a ruthless force,
Into the solemn church, and scatter the congregation,
Into the school where the scholar is studying;
Leave not the bridegroom quiet—no happiness must he have now with his bride,
Nor the peaceful farmer any peace, ploughing his field or gathering his grain,
So fierce you whirr and pound you drums—so shrill you bugles blow.

Beat! beat! drums!—blow! bugles! blow!
Over the traffic of cities—over the rumble of wheels in the streets;
Are beds prepared for sleepers at night in the houses? no sleepers must sleep in those beds,
No bargainers' bargains by day—no brokers or speculators —would they continue?
Would the talkers be talking? would the singer attempt to sing?
Would the lawyer rise in the court to state his case before the judge?
Then rattle quicker, heavier drums—you bugles wilder blow.

Beat! beat! drums!—blow! bugles! blow!
Make no parley—stop for no expostulation,

Mind not the timid—mind not the weeper or prayer,
Mind not the old man beseeching the young man,
Let not the child's voice be heard, nor the mother's en-
treaties,
Make even the trestles to shake the dead where they lie
awaiting the hearses,
So strong you thump O terrible drums—so loud you bugles
blow.


FROM PAUMANOK STARTING I FLY LIKE A BIRD

From Paumanok starting I fly like a bird,
Around and around to soar to sing the idea of all,
To the north betaking myself to sing their arctic songs,
To Kanada till I absorb Kanada in myself, to Michigan then,
To Wisconsin, Iowa, Minnesota, to sing their songs, (they
are inimitable;)
Then to Ohio and Indiana to sing theirs, to Missouri and
Kansas and Arkansas to sing theirs,
To Tennessee and Kentucky, to the Carolinas and Georgia
to sing theirs,
To Texas and so along up toward California, to roam
accepted everywhere;
To sing first, (to the tap of the war-drum if need be,)
The idea of all, of the Western world one and inseparable,
And then the song of each member of these States.

# SONG OF THE BANNER AT DAYBREAK

*Poet*

O a new song, a free song,
Flapping, flapping, flapping, flapping, by sounds, by voices
      clearer,
By the wind's voice and that of the drum,
By the banner's voice and child's voice and sea's voice and
      father's voice,
Low on the ground and high in the air,
On the ground where father and child stand,
In the upward air where their eyes turn,
Where the banner at daybreak is flapping.

Words! book-words! what are you?
Words no more, for harken and see,
My song is there in the open air, and I must sing,
With the banner and pennant a-flapping.

I'll weave the chord and twine in,
Man's desire and babe's desire, I'll twine them in, I'll put
      in life,
I'll put the bayonet's flashing point, I'll let bullets and slugs
      whizz,
(As one carrying a symbol and menace far into the future,
Crying with trumpet voice, *Arouse and beware! Beware and
      arouse!*)
I'll pour the verse with streams of blood, full of volition,
      full of joy,

233

Then loosen, launch forth, to go and compete,
With the banner and pennant a-flapping.


### Pennant

Come up here, bard, bard,
Come up here, soul, soul,
Come up here, dear little child,
To fly in the clouds and winds with me, and play with the
        measureless light.


### Child

Father what is that in the sky beckoning to me with long
        finger?
And what does it say to me all the while?


### Father

Nothing my babe you see in the sky,
And nothing at all to you it says—but look you my babe,
Look at these dazzling things in the houses, and see you the
        money-shops opening,
And see you the vehicles preparing to crawl along the streets
        with goods;
These, ah these, how valued and toil'd for these!
How envied by all the earth.

## Poet

Fresh and rosy red the sun is mounting high,
On floats the sea in distant blue careering through its
      channels,
On floats the wind over the breast of the sea setting in
      toward land,
The great steady wind from west or west-by-south,
Floating so buoyant with milk-white foam on the waters.

But I am not the sea nor the red sun,
I am not the wind with girlish laughter,
Not the immense wind which strengthens, not the wind
      which lashes,
Not the spirit that ever lashes its own body to terror and
      death,
But I am that which unseen comes and sings, sings, sings,
Which babbles in brooks and scoots in showers on the land,
Which the birds know in the woods mornings and evenings,
And the shore-sands know and the hissing wave, and that
      banner and pennant,
Aloft there flapping and flapping.

## Child

O father it is alive—it is full of people—it has children,
O now it seems to me it is talking to its children,
I hear it—it talks to me—O it is wonderful!
O it stretches—it spreads and runs so fast—O my father,
It is so broad it covers the whole sky.

235

## Father

Cease, cease, my foolish babe,
What you are saying is sorrowful to me, much it displeases
      me;
Behold with the rest again I say, behold not banners and
      pennants aloft,
But the well-prepared pavements behold, and mark the
      solid-wall'd houses.


## Banner and Pennant

Speak to the child O bard out of Manhattan,
To our children all, or north or south of Manhattan,
Point this day, leaving all the rest, to us over all—and yet
      we know not why,
For what are we, mere strips of cloth profiting nothing,
Only flapping in the wind?


## Poet

I hear and see not strips of cloth alone,
I hear the tramp of armies, I hear the challenging sentry,
I hear the jubilant shouts of millions of men, I hear Liberty!
I hear the drums beat and the trumpets blowing,
I myself move abroad swift-rising flying then,
I use the wings of the land-bird and use the wings of the
      sea-bird, and look down as from a height,
I do not deny the precious results of peace, I see populous
      cities with wealth incalculable,

I see numberless farms, I see the farmers working in their
        fields or barns,
I see mechanics working, I see buildings everywhere
        founded, going up, or finish'd,
I see trains of cars swiftly speeding along railroad tracks
        drawn by the locomotives,
I see the stores, depots, of Boston, Baltimore, Charleston,
        New Orleans,
I see far in the West the immense area of grain, I dwell
        awhile hovering,
I pass to the lumber forests of the North, and again to the
        Southern plantation, and again to California;
Sweeping the whole I see the countless profit, the busy
        gatherings, earn'd wages,
See the Identity formed out of thirty-eight spacious and
        haughty States, (and many more to come,)
See forts on the shores of harbors, see ships sailing in and
        out;
Then over all, (aye! aye!) my little and lengthen'd pen-
        nant shaped like a sword,
Runs swiftly up indicating war and defiance—and now the
        halyards have rais'd it,
Side of my banner broad and blue, side of my starry banner,
Discarding peace over all the sea and land.


## Banner and Pennant

Yet louder, higher, stronger, bard! yet farther, wider cleave!
No longer let our children deem us riches and peace alone,

We may be terror and carnage, and are so now,
Not now are we any one of these spacious and haughty
       States, (not any five, nor ten,)
Nor market nor depot we, nor money-bank in the city,
But these and all, and the brown and spreading land, and
       the mines below, are ours,
And the shores of the sea are ours, and the rivers great and
       small,
And the fields they moisten, and the crops and the fruits are
       ours,
Bays and channels and ships sailing in and out are ours—
       while we over all,
Over the area spread below, the three or four millions of
       square miles, the capitals,
The forty millions of people,—O bard! in life and death
       supreme,
We, even we, henceforth flaunt out masterful, high up
       above,
Not for the present alone, for a thousand years chanting
       through you,
This song to the soul of one poor little child.


### Child

O my father I like not the houses,
They will never to me be any thing, nor do I like money,
But to mount up there I would like, O father dear, that
       banner I like,
That pennant I would be and must be.

## Father

Child of mine you fill me with anguish,
To be that pennant would be too fearful,
Little you know what it is this day, and after this day,
     forever,
It is to gain nothing, but risk and defy every thing,
Forward to stand in front of wars—and O, such wars!—
     what have you to do with them?
With passions of demons, slaughter, premature death?


## Banner

Demons and death then I sing,
But in all, aye all will I, sword-shaped pennant for war,
And a pleasure new and ecstatic, and the prattled yearning
     of children,
Blent with the sounds of the peaceful land and the liquid
     wash of the sea,
And the black ships fighting on the sea envelop'd in smoke,
And the icy cool of the far, far north, with rustling cedars
     and pines,
And the whirr of drums and the sound of soldiers marching,
     and the hot sun shining south,
And the beach-waves combing over the beach on my Eastern
     shore, and my Western shore the same,
And all between those shores, and my ever running Missis-
     sippi with bends and chutes,

And my Illinois fields, and my Kansas fields, and my fields
of Missouri,
The Continent, devoting the whole identity without reserv-
ing an atom,
Pour in! whelm that which asks, which sings, with all and
the yield of all,
Fusing and holding, claiming, devouring the whole,
No more with tender lip, nor musical labial sound,
But out of the night emerging for good, our voice persuasive
no more,
Croaking like crows here in the wind.


*Poet*

My limbs, my veins dilate, my theme is clear at last,
Banner so broad advancing out of the night, I sing you
haughty and resolute,
I burst through where I waited long, too long, deafen'd and
blinded,
My hearing and tongue are come to me, (a little child taught
me,)
I hear from above O pennant of war you ironical call and
demand,
Insensate! insensate! (yet I at any rate chant you,) O banner!
Not houses of peace indeed are you, nor any nor all their
prosperity, (if need be, you shall again have every
one of those houses to destroy them,
You thought not to destroy those valuable houses, standing,
fast, full of comfort, built with money,

May they stand fast, then? not an hour except you
    above them and all stand fast;)
O banner, not money so precious are you, not farm produce
    you, nor the material good nutriment,
Nor excellent stores, nor landed on wharves from the ships,
Not the superb ships with sail-power or steam-power, fetch-
    ing and carrying cargoes,
Nor machinery, vehicles, trade, nor revenues—but you as
    henceforth I see you,
Running up out of the night, bringing your cluster of
    stars, (ever-enlarging stars,)
Divider of daybreak you, cutting the air, touch'd by the
    sun, measuring the sky,
(Passionately seen and yearn'd for by one poor little child,
While others remain busy or smartly talking, forever teach-
    ing thrift, thrift;)
O you up there! O pennant! where you undulate like a
    snake hissing so curious,
Out of reach, an idea only, yet furiously fought for, risking
    bloody death, loved by me,
So loved—O you banner leading the day with stars brought
    from the night!
Valueless, object of eyes, over all and demanding all—
    (absolute owner of all)—O banner and pennant!
I too leave the rest—great as it is, it is nothing—houses,
    machines are nothing—I see them not,
I see but you, O warlike pennant! O banner so broad, with
    stripes, I sing you only,
Flapping up there in the wind.

# RISE O DAYS FROM YOUR FATHOMLESS DEEPS

## I

Rise O days from your fathomless deeps, till you loftier,
    fiercer sweep,
Long for my soul hungering gymnastic I devour'd what
    the earth gave me,
Long I roam'd the woods of the north, long I watch'd
    Niagara pouring,
I travel'd the prairies over and slept on their breast, I cross'd
    the Nevadas, I cross'd the plateaus,
I ascended the towering rocks along the Pacific, I sail'd out
    to sea,
I sail'd through the storm, I was refresh'd by the storm,
I watch'd with joy the threatening maws of the waves,
I mark'd the white combs where they career'd so high,
    curling over,
I heard the wind piping, I saw the black clouds,
Saw from below what arose and mounted, (O superb! O
    wild as my heart, and powerful!)
Heard the continuous thunder as it bellow'd after the
    lightning,
Noted the slender and jagged threads of lightning as sud-
    den and fast amid the din they chased each other
    across the sky;
These, and such as these, I, elate, saw—saw with wonder,
    yet pensive and masterful,
All the menacing might of the globe uprisen around me,
Yet there with my soul I fed, I fed content, supercilious.

'Twas well, O soul—'twas a good preparation you gave me,
Now we advance our latent and ampler hunger to fill,
Now we go forth to receive what the earth and the sea
never gave us,
Not through the mighty woods we go, but through the
mightier cities,
Something for us is pouring now more than Niagara
pouring,
Torrents of men, (sources and rills of the Northwest are
you indeed inexhaustible?)
What, to pavements and homesteads here, what were those
storms of the mountains and sea?
What, to passions I witness around me to-day? was the sea
risen?
Was the wind piping the pipe of death under the black
clouds?
Lo! from deeps more unfathomable, something more deadly
and savage,
Manhattan rising, advancing with menacing front—Cin-
cinnati, Chicago, unchain'd;
What was that swell I saw on the ocean? behold what comes
here,
How it climbs with daring feet and hands—how it dashes!
How the true thunder bellows after the lightning—how
bright the flashes of lightning!
How Democracy with desperate vengeful port strides on,
shown through the dark by those flashes of light-
ning!

(Yet a mournful wail and low sob I fancied I heard through
the dark,
In a lull of the deafening confusion.)


3

Thunder on! stride on, Democracy! strike with vengeful
stroke!
And do you rise higher than ever yet O days, O cities!
Crash heavier, heavier yet O storms! you have done me
good,
My soul prepared in the mountains absorbs your immortal
strong nutriment,
Long had I walk'd my cities, my country roads through
farms, only half satisfied,
One doubt nauseous undulating like a snake, crawl'd on
the ground before me,
Continually preceding my steps, turning upon me oft,
ironically hissing low;
The cities I loved so well I abandon'd and left, I sped to
the certainties suitable to me,
Hungering, hungering, hungering, for primal energies and
Nature's dauntlessness,
I refresh'd myself with it only, I could relish it only,
I waited the bursting forth of the pent fire—on the water
and air I waited long;
But now I no longer wait, I am fully satisfied, I am glutted,
I have witness'd the true lightning, I have witness'd my
cities electric,

I have lived to behold man burst forth and warlike America
      rise,
Hence I will seek no more the food of the northern solitary
      wilds,
No more the mountains roam or sail the stormy sea.


## VIRGINIA—THE WEST

The noble sire fallen on evil days,
I saw with hand uplifted, menacing, brandishing,
(Memories of old in abeyance, love and faith in abeyance,)
The insane knife toward the Mother of All.

The noble son on sinewy feet advancing,
I saw, out of the land of prairies, land of Ohio's waters and
      of Indiana,
To the rescue the stalwart giant hurry his plenteous off-
      spring,
Drest in blue, bearing their trusty rifles on their shoulders.

Then the Mother of All with calm voice speaking,
As to you Rebellious, (I seemed to hear her say,) why
      strive against me, and why seek my life?
When you yourself forever provide to defend me?
For you provided me Washington—and now these also.

# CITY OF SHIPS

City of ships!
(O the black ships! O the fierce ships!
O the beautiful sharp-bow'd steam-ships and sail-ships!)
City of the world! (for all races are here,
All the lands of the earth make contributions here;)
City of the sea! city of hurried and glittering tides!
City whose gleeful tides continually rush or recede, whirling
      in and out with eddies and foam!
City of wharves and stores—city of tall facades of marble
      and iron!
Proud and passionate city—mettlesome, mad, extravagant
      city!
Spring up O city—not for peace alone, but be indeed your-
      self, warlike!
Fear not—submit to no models but your own O city!
Behold me—incarnate me as I have incarnated you!
I have rejected nothing you offer'd me—whom you adopted
      I have adopted,
Good or bad I never question you—I love all—I do not
      condemn any thing,
I chant and celebrate all that is yours—yet peace no more,
In peace I chanted peace, but now the drum of war is
      mine,
War, red war is my song through your streets, O city!

# THE CENTENARIAN'S STORY

*Volunteer of* 1861-2,
*(at Washington Park, Brooklyn, assisting the Centenarian.)*

Give me your hand old Revolutionary,
The hill-top is nigh, but a few steps, (make room gentle-
    men,)
Up the path you have follow'd me well, spite of your hun-
    dred and extra years,
You can walk old man, though your eyes are almost done,
Your faculties serve you, and presently I must have them
    serve me.

Rest, while I tell what the crowd around us means,
On the plain below recruits are drilling and exercising,
There is the camp, one regiment departs to-morrow,
Do you hear the officers giving their orders?
Do you hear the clank of the muskets?

Why what comes over you now old man?
Why do you tremble and clutch my hand so convulsively?
The troops are but drilling, they are yet surrounded with
    smiles,
Around them at hand the well-drest friends and the women,
While splendid and warm the afternoon sun shines down,
Green the midsummer verdure and fresh blows the dallying
    breeze,
O'er proud and peaceful cities and arm of the sea between.

But drill and parade are over, they march back to quarters,
Only hear that approval of hands! hear what a clapping!

As wending the crowds now part and disperse—but we old
      man,
Not for nothing have I brought you hither—we must re-
      main,
You to speak in your turn, and I to listen and tell.


### The Centenarian

When I clutch'd your hand it was not with terror,
But suddenly pouring about me here on every side,
And below there where the boys were drilling, and up the
      slopes they ran,
And where tents are pitch'd, and wherever you see south
      and south-east and south-west,
Over hills, across lowlands, and in the skirts of woods,
And along the shores, in mire (now fill'd over) came again
      and suddenly raged,
As eighty-five years a-gone no mere parade receiv'd with
      applause of friends,
But a battle which I took part in myself—aye, long ago as
      it is, I took part in it,
Walking then this hilltop, this same ground.

Aye, this is the ground,
My blind eyes even as I speak behold it re-peopled from
      graves,

The years recede, pavements and stately houses disappear,
Rude forts appear again, the old hoop'd guns are mounted,
I see the lines of rais'd earth stretching from river to bay,
I mark the vista of waters, I mark the uplands and slopes;
Here we lay encamp'd, it was this time in summer also.

As I talk I remember all, I remember the Declaration,
It was read here, the whole army paraded, it was read to us
       here,
By his staff surrounded the General stood in the middle, he
       held up his unsheath'd sword,
It glitter'd in the sun in full sight of the army.

'Twas a bold act then—the English war-ships had just
       arrived,
We could watch down the lower bay where they lay at
       anchor,
And the transports swarming with soldiers.

A few days more and they landed, and then the battle.

Twenty thousand were brought against us,
A veteran force furnish'd with good artillery.

I tell not now the whole of the battle,
But one brigade early in the forenoon order'd forward to
       engage the red-coats,
Of that brigade I tell, and how steadily it march'd,
And how long and well it stood confronting death.

Who do you think that was marching steadily sternly con-
fronting death?

It was the brigade of the youngest men, two thousand
strong,

Rais'd in Virginia and Maryland, and most of them known
personally to the General.


Jauntily forward they went with quick step toward
Gowanus' waters,

Till of a sudden unlook'd for by defiles through the woods,
gain'd at night,

The British advancing, rounding in from the east, fiercely
playing their guns,

That brigade of the youngest was cut off and at the enemy's
mercy.


The General watch'd them from this hill,

They made repeated desperate attempts to burst their en-
vironment,

Then drew close together, very compact, their flag flying in
the middle,

But O from the hills how the cannon were thinning and
thinning them!


It sickens me yet, that slaughter!

I saw the moisture gather in drops on the face of the
General,

I saw how he wrung his hands in anguish.

Meanwhile the British manœuvr'd to draw us out for a
      pitch'd battle,
But we dared not trust the chances of a pitch'd battle.

We fought the fight in detachments,
Sallying forth we fought at several points, but in each the
      luck was against us,
Our foe advancing, steadily getting the best of it, push'd us
      back to the works on this hill,
Till we turn'd menacing here, and then he left us.

That was the going out of the brigade of the youngest men,
      two thousand strong,
Few return'd, nearly all remain in Brooklyn.

That and here my General's first battle,
No women looking on nor sunshine to bask in, it did not
      conclude with applause,
Nobody clapp'd hands here then.

But in darkness in mist on the ground under a chill rain,
Wearied that night we lay foil'd and sullen,
While scornfully laugh'd many an arrogant lord against
      us encamp'd,
Quite within hearing, feasting, clinking wineglasses to-
      gether over their victory.

So dull and damp and another day,
But the night of that, mist lifting, rain ceasing,

Silent as a ghost while they thought they were sure of him,
  my General retreated.

I saw him at the river-side,
Down by the ferry lit by torches, hastening the embarcation;
My General waited till the soldiers and wounded were all
  pass'd over,
And then, (it was just sunrise,) these eyes rested on him
  for the last time.

Every one else seem'd fill'd with gloom,
Many no doubt thought of capitulation.

But when my General pass'd me,
As he stood in his boat and look'd toward the coming sun,
I saw something different from capitulation.


### Terminus

Enough, the Centenarian's story ends,
The two, the past and present, have interchanged,
I myself as connecter, as chansonnier of a great future, am
  now speaking.

And is this the ground Washington trod?
And these waters I listlessly daily cross, are these the waters
  he cross'd,
As resolute in defeat as other generals in their proudest
  triumphs?

252

I must copy the story, and send it eastward and westward,
I must preserve that look as it beam'd on you rivers of
Brooklyn.

See—as the annual round returns the phantoms return,
It is the 27th of August and the British have landed,
The battle begins and goes against us, behold through the
smoke Washington's face,
The brigade of Virginia and Maryland have march'd forth
to intercept the enemy,
They are cut off, murderous artillery from the hills plays
upon them,
Rank after rank falls, while over them silently droops the
flag,
Baptized that day in many a young man's bloody wounds,
In death, defeat, and sisters', mothers' tears.

Ah, hills and slopes of Brooklyn! I perceive you are more
valuable than your owners supposed;
In the midst of you stands an encampment very old,
Stands forever the camp of that dead brigade.


CAVALRY CROSSING A FORD

A line in long array where they wind betwixt green islands,
They take a serpentine course, their arms flash in the sun
—hark to the musical clank,

253

Behold the silvery river, in it the splashing horses loitering
      stop to drink,
Behold the brown-faced men, each group, each person a
      picture, the negligent rest on the saddles,
Some emerge on the opposite bank, others are just entering
      the ford—while,
Scarlet and blue and snowy white,
The guidon flags flutter gayly in the wind.


## BIVOUAC ON A MOUNTAIN SIDE

I see before me now a traveling army halting,
Below a fertile valley spread, with barns and the orchards
      of summer,
Behind, the terraced sides of a mountain, abrupt, in places
      rising high,
Broken, with rocks, with clinging cedars, with tall shapes
      dingily seen,
The numerous camp-fires scatter'd near and far, some away
      up on the mountain,
The shadowy forms of men and horses, looming, large-
      sized, flickering,
And over all the sky—the sky! far, far out of reach, studded,
      breaking out, the eternal stars.

# AN ARMY CORPS ON THE MARCH

With its cloud of skirmishers in advance,
With now the sound of a single shot snapping like a whip,
      and now an irregular volley,
The swarming ranks press on and on, the dense brigades
      press on,
Glittering dimly, toiling under the sun—the dust-cover'd
      men,
In columns rise and fall to the undulations of the ground,
With artillery interspers'd—the wheels rumble, the horses
      sweat,
As the army corps advances.


# BY THE BIVOUAC'S FITFUL FLAME

By the bivouac's fitful flame,
A procession winding around me, solemn and sweet and
      slow—but first I note,
The tents of the sleeping army, the fields' and woods' dim
      outline,
The darkness lit by spots of kindled fire, the silence,
Like a phantom far or near an occasional figure moving,
The shrubs and trees, (as I lift my eyes they seem to be
      stealthily watching me,)
While wind in procession thoughts, O tender and wondrous
      thoughts,

255

Of life and death, of home and the past and loved, and of
those that are far away;
A solemn and slow procession there as I sit on the ground,
By the bivouac's fitful flame.


## COME UP FROM THE FIELDS FATHER

Come up from the fields father, here's a letter from our
Pete,
And come to the front door mother, here's a letter from thy
dear son.


Lo, 'tis autumn,
Lo, where the trees, deeper green, yellower and redder,
Cool and sweeten Ohio's villages with leaves fluttering in
the moderate wind,
Where apples ripe in the orchards hang and grapes on the
trellis'd vines,
(Smell you the smell of the grapes on the vines?
Smell you the buckwheat where the bees were lately
buzzing?)


Above all, lo, the sky so calm, so transparent after the rain,
and with wondrous clouds,
Below too, all calm, all vital and beautiful, and the farm
prospers well.

256

Down in the fields all prospers well,
But now from the fields come father, come at the daughter's
     call,
And come to the entry mother, to the front door come right
     away.


Fast as she can she hurries, something ominous, her steps
     trembling,
She does not tarry to smooth her hair nor adjust her cap.


Open the envelope quickly,
O this is not our son's writing, yet his name is sign'd,
O a strange hand writes for our dear son, O stricken
     mother's soul!
All swims before her eyes, flashes with black, she catches
     the main words only,
Sentences broken, *gunshot wound in the breast, cavalry
     skirmish, taken to hospital,*
*At present low, but will soon be better.*


Ah now the single figure to me,
Amid all teeming and wealthy Ohio with all its cities and
     farms,
Sickly white in the face and dull in the head, very faint,
By the jamb of a door leans.


*Grieve not so, dear mother,* (the just-grown daughter speaks
     through her sobs,

The little sisters huddle around speechless and dismay'd,)
*See, dearest mother, the letter says Pete will soon be better.*

Alas poor boy, he will never be better, (nor may-be needs to
      be better, that brave and simple soul,)
While they stand at home at the door he is dead already,
The only son is dead.

But the mother needs to be better,
She with thin form presently drest in black,
By day her meals untouch'd, then at night fitfully sleeping,
      often waking,
In the midnight waking, weeping, longing with one deep
      longing,
O that she might withdraw unnoticed, silent from life
      escape and withdraw,
To follow, to seek, to be with her dear dead son.

## VIGIL STRANGE I KEPT ON THE FIELD
## ONE NIGHT

Vigil strange I kept on the field one night;
When you my son and my comrade dropt at my side that day,
One look I but gave which your dear eyes return'd with a
      look I shall never forget,
One touch of your hand to mine O boy, reach'd up as you
      lay on the ground,

Then onward I sped in the battle, the even-contested battle,
Till late in the night reliev'd to the place at last again I
      made my way,
Found you in death so cold dear comrade, found your body
      son of responding kisses, (never again on earth
      responding,)
Bared your face in the starlight, curious the scene, cool blew
      the moderate night-wind,
Long there and then in vigil I stood, dimly around me the
      battle-field spreading,
Vigil wondrous and vigil sweet there in the fragrant silent
      night,
But not a tear fell, not even a long-drawn sigh, long, long I
      gazed,
Then on the earth partially reclining sat by your side lean-
      ing my chin in my hands,
Passing sweet hours, immortal and mystic hours with you
      dearest comrade—not a tear, not a word,
Vigil of silence, love and death, vigil for you my son and
      my soldier,
As onward silently stars aloft, eastward new ones upward
      stole,
Vigil final for you brave boy, (I could not save you, swift
      was your death,
I faithfully loved you and cared for you living, I think we
      shall surely meet again,)
Till at latest lingering of the night, indeed just as the dawn
      appear'd,
My comrade I wrapt in his blanket, envelop'd well his
      form,

Folded the blanket well, tucking it carefully over head and
carefully under feet,
And there and then and bathed by the rising sun, my son in
his grave, in his rude-dug grave I deposited,
Ending my vigil strange with that, vigil of night and battle-
field dim,
Vigil for boy of responding kisses, (never again on earth
responding,)
Vigil for comrade swiftly slain, vigil I never forget, how as
day brighten'd,
I rose from the chill ground and folded my soldier well in
his blanket,
And buried him where he fell.


## A MARCH IN THE RANKS HARD-PREST, AND THE
## ROAD UNKNOWN

A march in the ranks hard-prest, and the road unknown,
A route through a heavy wood with muffled steps in the
darkness,
Our army foil'd with loss severe, and the sullen remnant
retreating,
Till after midnight glimmer upon us the lights of a dim-
lighted building,
We come to an open space in the woods, and halt by the
dim-lighted building,
'Tis a large old church at the crossing roads, now an im-
promptu hospital,

Entering but for a minute I see a sight beyond all the
 pictures and poems ever made,
Shadows of deepest, deepest black, just lit by moving
 candles and lamps,
And by one great pitchy torch stationary with wild red flame
 and clouds of smoke,
By these, crowds, groups of forms vaguely I see on the floor,
 some in the pews laid down,
At my feet more distinctly a soldier, a mere lad, in danger
 of bleeding to death, (he is shot in the abdomen,)
I stanch the blood temporarily, (the youngster's face is
 white as a lily,)
Then before I depart I sweep my eyes o'er the scene fain
 to absorb it all,
Faces, varieties, postures beyond description, most in ob-
 scurity, some of them dead,
Surgeons operating, attendants holding lights, the smell of
 ether, the odor of blood,
The crowd, O the crowd of the bloody forms, the yard out-
 side also fill'd,
Some on the bare ground, some on planks or stretchers, some
 in the death-spasm sweating,
An occasional scream or cry, the doctor's shouted orders or
 calls,
The glisten of the little steel instruments catching the glint
 of the torches,
These I resume as I chant, I see again the forms, I smell the
 odor,
Then hear outside the orders given, *Fall in, my men, fall in;*

But first I bend to the dying lad, his eyes open, a half-smile
        gives he me,
Then the eyes close, calmly close, and I speed forth to the
        darkness,
Resuming, marching, ever in darkness marching, on in the
        ranks,
The unknown road still marching.

## A SIGHT IN CAMP IN THE DAYBREAK GRAY AND DIM

A sight in camp in the daybreak gray and dim,
As from my tent I emerge so early sleepless,
As slow I walk in the cool fresh air the path near by the
        hospital tent,
Three forms I see on stretchers lying, brought out there
        untended lying,
Over each the blanket spread, ample brownish woolen
        blanket,
Gray and heavy blanket, folding, covering all.

Curious I halt and silent stand,
Then with light fingers I from the face of the nearest the
        first just lift the blanket;
Who are you elderly man so gaunt and grim, with well-
        gray'd hair, and flesh all sunken about the eyes?
Who are you my dear comrade?

Then to the second I step—and who are you my child and
        darling?
Who are you sweet boy with cheeks yet blooming?

Then to the third—a face nor child nor old, very calm, as
        of beautiful yellow-white ivory;
Young man I think I know you—I think this face is the
        face of the Christ himself,
Dead and divine and brother of all, and here again he lies.


## AS TOILSOME I WANDER'D VIRGINIA'S WOODS

As toilsome I wander'd Virginia's woods,
To the music of rustling leaves kick'd by my feet, (for 'twas
        autumn,)
I mark'd at the foot of a tree the grave of a soldier;
Mortally wounded he and buried on the retreat, (easily all
        could I understand,)
The halt of a mid-day hour, when up! no time to lose—yet
        this sign left,
On a tablet scrawl'd and nail'd on the tree by the grave,
*Bold, cautious, true, and my loving comrade.*

Long, long I muse, then on my way go wandering,
Many a changeful season to follow, and many a scene of
        life,
Yet at times through changeful season and scene, abrupt,
        alone, or in the crowded street,

Comes before me the unknown soldier's grave, comes the
    inscription rude in Virginia's woods,
*Bold, cautious, true, and my loving comrade.*


## NOT THE PILOT

Not the pilot has charged himself to bring his ship into
        port, though beaten back and many times baffled;
Not the pathfinder penetrating inland weary and long,
By deserts parch'd, snows chill'd, rivers wet, perseveres till
        he reaches his destination,
More than I have charged myself, heeded or unheeded, to
        compose a march for these States,
For a battle-call, rousing to arms if need be, years, centuries
        hence.


## YEAR THAT TREMBLED AND REEL'D
## BENEATH ME

Year that trembled and reel'd beneath me!
Your summer wind was warm enough, yet the air I breathed
        froze me,
A thick gloom fell through the sunshine and darken'd me,
Must I change my triumphant songs? said I to myself,
Must I indeed learn to chant the cold dirges of the baffled?
And sullen hymns of defeat?

# THE WOUND-DRESSER

## 1

An old man bending I come among new faces,
Years looking backward resuming in answer to children,
Come tell us old man, as from young men and maidens
      that love me,
(Arous'd and angry, I'd thought to beat the alarum, and
      urge relentless war,
But soon my fingers fail'd me, my face droop'd and I
      resign'd myself,
To sit by the wounded and soothe them, or silently watch
      the dead;)
Years hence of these scenes, of these furious passions, these
      chances,
Of unsurpass'd heroes, (was one side so brave? the other
      was equally brave;)
Now be witness again, paint the mightiest armies of earth,
Of those armies so rapid so wondrous what saw you to tell
      us?
What stays with you latest and deepest? of curious panics,
Of hard-fought engagements or sieges tremendous what
      deepest remains?

## 2

O maidens and young men I love and that love me,
What you ask of my days those the strangest and sudden
     your talking recalls,

Soldier alert I arrive after a long march cover'd with sweat
and dust,
In the nick of time I come, plunge in the fight, loudly shout
in the rush of successful charge,
Enter the captur'd works—yet lo, like a swift-running river
they fade,
Pass and are gone they fade—I dwell not on soldiers' perils
or soldiers' joys,
(Both I remember well—many the hardships, few the
joys, yet I was content.)


But in silence, in dreams' projections,
While the world of gain and appearance and mirth goes on,
So soon what is over forgotten, and waves wash the imprints
off the sand,
With hinged knees returning I enter the doors, (while for
you up there,
Whoever you are, follow without noise and be of strong
heart.)


Bearing the bandages, water and sponge,
Straight and swift to my wounded I go,
Where they lie on the ground after the battle brought in,
Where their priceless blood reddens the grass the ground,
Or to the rows of the hospital tent, or under the roof'd
hospital,
To the long rows of cots up and down each side I return,
To each and all one after another I draw near, not one do
I miss,

An attendant follows holding a tray, he carries a refuse pail,
Soon to be fill'd with clotted rags and blood, emptied, and
        fill'd again.

I onward go, I stop,
With hinged knees and steady hand to dress wounds,
I am firm with each, the pangs are sharp yet unavoidable,
One turns to me his appealing eyes—poor boy! I never
        knew you,
Yet I think I could not refuse this moment to die for you,
        if that would save you.


3

On, on I go, (open doors of time! open hospital doors!)
The crush'd head I dress, (poor crazed hand tear not the
        bandage away,)
The neck of the cavalry-man with the bullet through and
        through I examine,
Hard the breathing rattles, quite glazed already the eye, yet
        life struggles hard,
(Come sweet death! be persuaded O beautiful death!
In mercy come quickly.)

From the stump of the arm, the amputated hand,
I undo the clotted lint, remove the slough, wash off the
        matter and blood,
Back on his pillow the soldier bends with curv'd neck and
        side-falling head,

His eyes are closed, his face is pale, he dares not look on the
        bloody stump,
And has not yet look'd on it.


I dress a wound in the side, deep, deep,
But a day or two more, for see the frame all wasted and
        sinking,
And the yellow-blue countenance see.


I dress the perforated shoulder, the foot with the bullet-
        wound,
Cleanse the one with a gnawing and putrid gangrene, so
        sickening, so offensive,
While the attendant stands behind aside me holding the
        tray and pail.


I am faithful, I do not give out,
The fractur'd thigh, the knee, the wound in the abdomen,
These and more I dress with impassive hand, (yet deep in
        my breast a fire, a burning flame.)


### 4

Thus in silence in dreams' projections,
Returning, resuming, I thread my way through the hospitals,
The hurt and wounded I pacify with soothing hand,
I sit by the restless all the dark night, some are so young,
Some suffer so much, I recall the experience sweet and sad,

(Many a soldier's loving arms about this neck have cross'd
and rested,
Many a soldier's kiss dwells on these bearded lips.)


## LONG, TOO LONG AMERICA

Long, too long America,
Traveling roads all even and peaceful you learn'd from joys
and prosperity only,
But now, ah now, to learn from crises of anguish, advanc-
ing, grappling with direst fate and recoiling not,
And now to conceive and show to the world what your
children en-masse really are,
(For who except myself has yet conceiv'd what your
children en-masse really are?)


## GIVE ME THE SPLENDID SILENT SUN

I

Give me the splendid silent sun with all his beams full-
dazzling,
Give me juicy autumnal fruit ripe and red from the orchard,
Give me a field where the unmow'd grass grows,
Give me an arbor, give me the trellis'd grape,
Give me fresh corn and wheat, give me serene-moving ani-
mals teaching content,

Give me nights perfectly quiet as on high plateaus west of
the Mississippi, and I looking up at the stars,
Give me odorous at sunrise a garden of beautiful flowers
where I can walk undisturb'd,
Give me for marriage a sweet-breath'd woman of whom I
should never tire,
Give me a perfect child, give me away aside from the noise
of the world a rural domestic life,
Give me to warble spontaneous songs recluse by myself, for
my own ears only,
Give me solitude, give me Nature, give me again O Nature
your primal sanities!


These demanding to have them, (tired with ceaseless excite-
ment, and rack'd by the war-strife,)
These to procure incessantly asking, rising in cries from my
heart,
While yet incessantly asking still I adhere to my city,
Day upon day and year upon year O city, walking your
streets,
Where you hold me enchain'd a certain time refusing to give
me up,
Yet giving to make me glutted, enrich'd of soul, you give
me forever faces;
(O I see what I sought to escape, confronting, reversing my
cries,
I see my own soul trampling down what it ask'd for.)

Keep your splendid silent sun,

Keep your woods O Nature, and the quiet places by the
woods,

Keep your fields of clover and timothy, and your corn-fields
and orchards,

Keep the blossoming buckwheat fields where the Ninth-
month bees hum;

Give me faces and streets—give me these phantoms inces-
sant and endless along the trottoirs!

Give me interminable eyes—give me women—give me
comrades and lovers by the thousand!

Let me see new ones every day—let me hold new ones by
the hand every day!

Give me such shows—give me the streets of Manhattan!

Give me Broadway, with the soldiers marching—give me
the sound of the trumpets and drums!

(The soldiers in companies or regiments—some starting
away, flush'd and reckless,

Some, their time up, returning with thinn'd ranks, young,
yet very old, worn, marching, noticing nothing;)

Give me the shores and wharves heavy-fringed with black
ships!

O such for me! O an intense life, full to repletion and varied!

The life of the theatre, bar-room, huge hotel, for me!

The saloon of the steamer! the crowded excursion for me!
the torchlight procession!

The dense brigade bound for the war, with high piled mili-
tary wagons following;

People, endless, streaming, with strong voices, passions,
      pageants,
Manhattan streets with their powerful throbs, with beating
      drums as now,
The endless and noisy chorus, the rustle and clank of mus-
      kets, (even the sight of the wounded,)
Manhattan crowds, with their turbulent musical chorus!
Manhattan faces and eyes forever for me.


## DIRGE FOR TWO VETERANS


    The last sunbeam
Lightly falls from the finish'd Sabbath,
On the pavement here, and there beyond it is looking,
    Down a new-made double grave.


    Lo, the moon ascending,
Up from the east the silvery round moon,
Beautiful over the house-tops, ghastly, phantom moon,
    Immense and silent moon.


    I see a sad procession,
And I hear the sound of coming full-key'd bugles,
All the channels of the city streets they're flooding,
    As with voices and with tears.

I hear the great drums pounding,
And the small drums steady whirring,
And every blow of the great convulsive drums,
    Strikes me through and through.


For the son is brought with the father,
(In the foremost ranks of the fierce assault they fell,
Two veterans son and father dropt together,
    And the double grave awaits them.)


Now near blow the bugles,
And the drums strike more convulsive,
And the daylight o'er the pavement quite has faded,
    And the strong dead-march enwraps me.


In the eastern sky up-buoying,
The sorrowful vast phantom moves illumin'd,
('Tis some mother's large transparent face,
    In heaven brighter growing.)


O strong dead-march you please me!
O moon immense with your silvery face you soothe me!
O my soldiers twain! O my veterans passing to burial!
    What I have I also give you.


The moon gives you light,
And the bugles and the drums give you music,
And my heart, O my soldiers, my veterans,
    My heart gives you love.

# OVER THE CARNAGE ROSE PROPHETIC
## A VOICE

Over the carnage rose prophetic a voice,
Be not dishearten'd, affection shall solve the problems of
      freedom yet,
Those who love each other shall become invincible,
They shall yet make Columbia victorious.

Sons of the Mother of All, you shall yet be victorious,
You shall yet laugh to scorn the attacks of all the remainder
      of the earth.

No danger shall balk Columbia's lovers,
If need be a thousand shall sternly immolate themselves for
      one.

One from Massachusetts shall be a Missourian's comrade,
From Maine and from hot Carolina, and another an Ore-
      gonese, shall be friends triune,
More precious to each other than all the riches of the earth.

To Michigan, Florida perfumes shall tenderly come,
Not the perfumes of flowers, but sweeter, and wafted be-
      yond death.

It shall be customary in the houses and streets to see manly
      affection,
The most dauntless and rude shall touch face to face lightly,

The dependence of Liberty shall be lovers,
The continuance of Equality shall be comrades.

These shall tie you and band you stronger than hoops of
      iron,
I, ecstatic, O partners! O lands! with the love of lovers tie
      you.

(Were you looking to be held together by lawyers?
Or by an agreement on a paper? or by arms?
Nay, nor the world, nor any living thing, will so cohere.)

## I SAW OLD GENERAL AT BAY

I saw old General at bay,
(Old as he was, his gray eyes yet shone out in battle like
      stars,)
His small force was now completely hemm'd in, in his
      works,
He call'd for volunteers to run the enemy's lines, a desperate
      emergency,
I saw a hundred and more step forth from the ranks, but two
      or three were selected,
I saw them receive their orders aside, they listen'd with care,
      the adjutant was very grave,
I saw them depart with cheerfulness, freely risking their
      lives.

# THE ARTILLERYMAN'S VISION

While my wife at my side lies slumbering, and the wars
  are over long,

And my head on the pillow rests at home, and the vacant
  midnight passes,

And through the stillness, through the dark, I hear, just
  hear, the breath of my infant,

There in the room as I wake from sleep this vision presses
  upon me;

The engagement opens there and then in fantasy unreal,

The skirmishers begin, they crawl cautiously ahead, I hear
  the irregular snap! snap!

I hear the sounds of the different missiles, the short *t-h-t!*
  *t-h-t!* of the rifle-balls,

I see the shells exploding leaving small white clouds, I hear
  the great shells shrieking as they pass,

The grape like the hum and whirr of wind through the trees,
  (tumultuous now the contest rages,)

All the scenes at the batteries rise in detail before me again,

The crashing and smoking, the pride of the men in their
  pieces,

The chief-gunner ranges and sights his piece and selects a
  fuse of the right time,

After firing I see him lean aside and look eagerly off to note
  the effect;

Elsewhere I hear the cry of a regiment charging, (the young
  colonel leads himself this time with brandish'd
  sword,)

I see the gaps cut by the enemy's volleys, (quickly fill'd up, no delay,)

I breathe the suffocating smoke, then the flat clouds hover low concealing all;

Now a strange lull for a few seconds, not a shot fired on either side,

Then resumed the chaos louder than ever, with eager calls and orders of officers,

While from some distant part of the field the wind wafts to my ears a shout of applause, (some special success,)

And ever the sound of the cannon far or near, (rousing even in dreams a devilish exultation and all the old mad joy in the depths of my soul,)

And ever the hastening of infantry shifting positions, batteries, cavalry, moving hither and thither,

(The falling, dying, I heed not, the wounded dripping and red I heed not, some to the rear are hobbling,)

Grime, heat, rush, aide-de-camps galloping by or on a full run,

With the patter of small arms, the warning *s-s-t* of the rifles, (these in my vision I hear or see,)

And bombs bursting in air, and at night the vari-color'd rockets.

# ETHIOPIA SALUTING THE COLORS

Who are you dusky woman, so ancient hardly human,
With your woolly-white and turban'd head, and bare bony
feet?
Why rising by the roadside here, do you the colors greet?

('Tis while our army lines Carolina's sands and pines,
Forth from thy hovel door thou Ethiopia com'st to me,
As under doughty Sherman I march toward the sea.)

*Me master years a hundred since from my parents sunder'd,*
*A little child, they caught me as the savage beast is caught,*
*Then hither me across the sea the cruel slaver brought.*

No further does she say, but lingering all the day,
Her high-borne turban'd head she wags, and rolls her dark-
ling eye,
And courtesies to the regiments, the guidons moving by.

What is it fateful woman, so blear, hardly human?
Why wag your head with turban bound, yellow, red and
green?
Are the things so strange and marvelous you see or have
seen?

# NOT YOUTH PERTAINS TO ME

Not youth pertains to me,
Nor delicatesse, I cannot beguile the time with talk,
Awkward in the parlor, neither a dancer nor elegant,
In the learn'd coterie sitting constrain'd and still, for learn-
        ing inures not to me,
Beauty, knowledge, inure not to me—yet there are two or
        three things inure to me,
I have nourish'd the wounded and sooth'd many a dying
        soldier,
And at intervals waiting or in the midst of camp,
Composed these songs.

# RACE OF VETERANS

Race of veterans—race of victors!
Race of the soil, ready for conflict—race of the conquering
        march!
(No more credulity's race, abiding-temper'd race,)
Race henceforth owning no law but the law of itself,
Race of passion and the storm.

# WORLD TAKE GOOD NOTICE

World take good notice, silver stars fading,
Milky hue ript, weft of white detaching,
Coals thirty-eight, baleful and burning,
Scarlet, significant, hands off warning,
Now and henceforth flaunt from these shores.

# O TAN-FACED PRAIRIE-BOY

O tan-faced prairie-boy,
Before you came to camp came many a welcome gift,
Praises and presents came and nourishing food, till at last
      among the recruits,
You came, taciturn, with nothing to give—we but look'd on
      each other,
When lo! more than all the gifts of the world you gave
      me.


# LOOK DOWN FAIR MOON

Look down fair moon and bathe this scene,
Pour softly down night's nimbus floods on faces ghastly,
      swollen, purple,
On the dead on their backs with arms toss'd wide,
Pour down your unstinted nimbus sacred moon.


# RECONCILIATION

Word over all, beautiful as the sky,
Beautiful that war and all its deeds of carnage must in time
      be utterly lost,
That the hands of the sisters Death and Night incessantly
      softly wash again, and ever again, this soil'd world;
For my enemy is dead, a man divine as myself is dead,

I look where he lies white-faced and still in the coffin—I
    draw near,
Bend down and touch lightly with my lips the white face in
    the coffin.


## HOW SOLEMN AS ONE BY ONE

*(Washington City, 1865.)*

How solemn as one by one,
As the ranks returning worn and sweaty, as the men file by
    where I stand,
As the faces the masks appear, as I glance at the faces study-
    ing the masks,
(As I glance upward out of this page studying you, dear
    friend, whoever you are,)
How solemn the thought of my whispering soul to each in
    the ranks, and to you,
I see behind each mask that wonder a kindred soul,
O the bullet could never kill what you really are, dear
    friend,
Nor the bayonet stab what you really are;
The soul! yourself I see, great as any, good as the best,
Waiting secure and content, which the bullet could never
    kill,
Nor the bayonet stab O friend.

## AS I LAY WITH MY HEAD IN YOUR LAP
## CAMERADO

As I lay with my head in your lap camerado,
The confession I made I resume, what I said to you and the
open air I resume,
I know I am restless and make others so,
I know my words are weapons full of danger, full of death,
For I confront peace, security, and all the settled laws, to
unsettle them,
I am more resolute because all have denied me than I could
ever have been had all accepted me,
I heed not and have never heeded either experience, cau-
tions, majorities, nor ridicule,
And the threat of what is call'd hell is little or nothing to me,
And the lure of what is call'd heaven is little or nothing to
me;
Dear camerado! I confess I have urged you onward with me,
and still urge you, without the least idea what is our
destination,
Or whether we shall be victorious, or utterly quell'd and
defeated.


## DELICATE CLUSTER

Delicate cluster! flag of teeming life!
Covering all my lands—all my seashores lining!
Flag of death! (how I watch'd you through the smoke of
battle pressing!

How I heard you flap and rustle, cloth defiant!)
Flag cerulean—sunny flag, with the orbs of night dappled!
Ah my silvery beauty—ah my woolly white and crimson!
Ah to sing the song of you, my matron mighty!
My sacred one, my mother.


## TO A CERTAIN CIVILIAN

Did you ask dulcet rhymes from me?
Did you seek the civilian's peaceful and languishing
      rhymes?
Did you find what I sang erewhile so hard to follow?
Why I was not singing erewhile for you to follow, to
      understand—nor am I now;
(I have been born of the same as the war was born,
The drum-corps' rattle is ever to me sweet music, I love
      well the martial dirge,
With slow wail and convulsive throb leading the officer's
      funeral;)
What to such as you anyhow such a poet as I? therefore
      leave my works,
And go lull yourself with what you can understand, and
      with piano tunes,
For I lull nobody, and you will never understand me.

# LO, VICTRESS ON THE PEAKS

Lo, Victress on the peaks,
Where thou with mighty brow regarding the world,
(The world O Libertad, that vainly conspired against thee,)
Out of its countless beleaguering toils, after thwarting them
     all,
Dominant, with the dazzling sun around thee,
Flauntest now unharm'd in immortal soundness and bloom
     —lo, in these hours supreme,
No poem proud, I chanting bring to thee, nor mastery's
     rapturous verse,
But a cluster containing night's darkness and blood-dripping
     wounds,
And psalms of the dead.


# SPIRIT WHOSE WORK IS DONE

### (*Washington City,* 1865.)

Spirit whose work is done—spirit of dreadful hours!
Ere departing fade from my eyes your forests of bayonets;
Spirit of gloomiest fears and doubts, (yet onward ever
     unfaltering pressing,)
Spirit of many a solemn day and many a savage scene—
     electric spirit,
That with muttering voice through the war now closed, like
     a tireless phantom flitted,

Rousing the land with breath of flame, while you beat and
       beat the drum,
Now as the sound of the drum, hollow and harsh to the
       last, reverberates round me,
As your ranks, your immortal ranks, return, return from
       the battles,
As the muskets of the young men yet lean over their
       shoulders,
As I look on the bayonets bristling over their shoulders,
As those slanted bayonets, whole forests of them appearing
       in the distance, approach and pass on, returning
       homeward,
Moving with steady motion, swaying to and fro to the
       right and left,
Evenly lightly rising and falling while the steps keep time;
Spirit of hours I knew, all hectic red one day, but pale as
       death next day,
Touch my mouth ere you depart, press my lips close,
Leave me your pulses of rage—bequeath them to me—fill
       me with currents convulsive,
Let them scorch and blister out of my chants when you are
       gone,
Let them identify you to the future in these songs.


## ADIEU TO A SOLDIER

Adieu O soldier,
You of the rude campaigning, (which we shared,)
The rapid march, the life of the camp,

285

The hot contention of opposing fronts, the long manœuvre,
Red battles with their slaughter, the stimulus, the strong
      terrific game,
Spell of all brave and manly hearts, the trains of time
      through you and like of you all fill'd,
With war and war's expression.

Adieu dear comrade,
Your mission is fulfill'd—but I, more warlike,
Myself and this contentious soul of mine,
Still on our own campaigning bound,
Through untried roads with ambushes opponents lined,
Through many a sharp defeat and many a crisis, often
      baffled,
Here marching, ever marching on, a war fight out—aye
      here,
To fiercer, weightier battles give expression.


## TURN O LIBERTAD

Turn O Libertad, for the war is over,
From it and all henceforth expanding, doubting no more,
      resolute, sweeping the world,
Turn from lands retrospective recording proofs of the
      past,
From the singers that sing the trailing glories of the past,
From the chants of the feudal world, the triumphs of kings,
      slavery, caste,

Turn to the world, the triumphs reserv'd and to come—
      give up that backward world,
Leave to the singers of hitherto, give them the trailing past,
But what remains remains for singers for you—wars to
      come are for you,
(Lo, how the wars of the past have duly inured to you, and
      the wars of the present also inure;)
Then turn, and be not alarm'd O Libertad—turn your
      undying face,
To where the future, greater than all the past,
Is swiftly, surely preparing for you.


## TO THE LEAVEN'D SOIL THEY TROD

To the leaven'd soil they trod calling I sing for the last,
(Forth from my tent emerging for good, loosing, untying
      the tent-ropes,)
In the freshness the forenoon air, in the far-stretching cir-
      cuits and vistas again to peace restored,
To the fiery fields emanative and the endless vistas beyond,
      to the South and the North,
To the leaven'd soil of the general Western world to
      attest my songs,
To the Alleghanian hills and the tireless Mississippi,
To the rocks I calling sing, and all the trees in the woods,
To the plains of the poems of heroes, to the prairies spread-
      ing wide,

To the far-off sea and the unseen winds, and the sane
      impalpable air;
And responding they answer all, (but not in words,)
The average earth, the witness of war and peace, acknowl-
      edges mutely,
The prairie draws me close, as the father to bosom broad
      the son,
The Northern ice and rain that began me nourish me to
      the end,
But the hot sun of the South is to fully ripen my songs.

# Memories
# of President Lincoln

## WHEN LILACS LAST IN THE DOORYARD
## BLOOM'D

### 1

When lilacs last in the dooryard bloom'd,
And the great star early droop'd in the western sky in the
     night,
I mourn'd, and yet shall mourn with ever-returning spring.

Ever-returning spring, trinity sure to me you bring,
Lilac blooming perennial and drooping star in the west,
And thought of him I love.

### 2

O powerful western fallen star!
O shades of night—O moody, tearful night!
O great star disappear'd—O the black murk that hides the
     star!

O cruel hands that hold me powerless—O helpless soul of
     me!
O harsh surrounding cloud that will not free my soul.


### 3

In the dooryard fronting an old farm-house near the white-
     wash'd palings,
Stands the lilac-bush tall-growing with heart-shaped leaves
     of rich green,
With many a pointed blossom rising delicate, with the
     perfume strong I love,
With every leaf a miracle—and from this bush in the door-
     yard,
With delicate-color'd blossoms and heart-shaped leaves of
     rich green,
A sprig with its flower I break.


### 4

In the swamp in secluded recesses,
A shy and hidden bird is warbling a song.

Solitary the thrush,
The hermit withdrawn to himself, avoiding the settlements,
Sings by himself a song.

Song of the bleeding throat,
Death's outlet song of life, (for well dear brother I know,
If thou wast not granted to sing thou would'st surely die.)

5

Over the breast of the spring, the land, amid cities,
Amid lanes and through old woods, where lately the violets
peep'd from the ground, spotting the gray debris,
Amid the grass in the fields each side of the lanes, passing
the endless grass,
Passing the yellow-spear'd wheat, every grain from its
shroud in the dark-brown fields uprisen,
Passing the apple-tree blows of white and pink in the
orchards,
Carrying a corpse to where it shall rest in the grave,
Night and day journeys a coffin.


6

Coffin that passes through lanes and streets,
Through day and night with the great cloud darkening the
land,
With the pomp of the inloop'd flags with the cities draped
in black,
With the show of the States themselves as of crape-veil'd
women standing,
With processions long and winding and the flambeaus of
the night,
With the countless torches lit, with the silent sea of faces
and the unbared heads,
With the waiting depot, the arriving coffin, and the sombre
faces,

With dirges through the night, with the thousand voices
      rising strong and solemn,
With all the mournful voices of the dirges pour'd around
      the coffin,
The dim-lit churches and the shuddering organs—where
      amid these you journey,
With the tolling tolling bells' perpetual clang,
Here, coffin that slowly passes,
I give you my sprig of lilac.


## 7

(Nor for you, for one alone,
Blossoms and branches green to coffins all I bring,
For fresh as the morning, thus would I chant a song for
      you O sane and sacred death.

All over bouquets of roses,
O death, I cover you over with roses and early lilies,
But mostly and now the lilac that blooms the first,
Copious I break, I break the sprigs from the bushes,
With loaded arms I come, pouring for you,
For you and the coffins all of you O death.)


## 8

O western orb sailing the heaven,
Now I know what you must have meant as a month since
      I walk'd,

As I walk'd in silence the transparent shadowy night,

As I saw you had something to tell as you bent to me night
       after night,

As you droop'd from the sky low down as if to my side,
       (while the other stars all look'd on,)

As we wander'd together the solemn night, (for some-
       thing I know not what kept me from sleep,)

As the night advanced, and I saw on the rim of the west how
       full you were of woe,

As I stood on the rising ground in the breeze in the cool
       transparent night,

As I watch'd where you pass'd and was lost in the nether-
       ward black of the night,

As my soul in its trouble dissatisfied sank, as where you
       sad orb,

Concluded, dropt in the night, and was gone.

9

Sing on there in the swamp,

O singer bashful and tender, I hear your notes, I hear your
       call,

I hear, I come presently, I understand you,

But a moment I linger, for the lustrous star has detain'd
       me,

The star my departing comrade holds and detains me.

## 10

O how shall I warble myself for the dead one there I loved?
And how shall I deck my song for the large sweet soul that
      has gone?
And what shall my perfume be for the grave of him I love?

Sea-winds blown from east and west,
Blown from the Eastern sea and blown from the Western
      sea, till there on the prairies meeting,
These and with these and the breath of my chant,
I'll perfume the grave of him I love.

## 11

O what shall I hang on the chamber walls?
And what shall the pictures be that I hang on the walls,
To adorn the burial-house of him I love?

Pictures of growing spring and farms and homes,
With the Fourth-month eve at sundown, and the gray
      smoke lucid and bright,
With floods of the yellow gold of the gorgeous, indolent,
      sinking sun, burning, expanding the air,
With the fresh sweet herbage under foot, and the pale
      green leaves of the trees prolific,
In the distance the flowing glaze, the breast of the river,
      with a wind-dapple here and there,
With ranging hills on the banks, with many a line against
    · the sky, and shadows,

And the city at hand with dwellings so dense, and stacks of
     chimneys,
And all the scenes of life and the workshops, and the work-
     men homeward returning.


12

Lo, body and soul—this land,
My own Manhattan with spires, and the sparkling and
     hurrying tides, and the ships,
The varied and ample land, the South and the North in
     the light, Ohio's shores and flashing Missouri,
And ever the far-spreading prairies cover'd with grass and
     corn.

Lo, the most excellent sun so calm and haughty,
The violet and purple morn with just-felt breezes,
The gentle soft-born measureless light,
The miracle spreading bathing all, the fulfill'd noon,
The coming eve delicious, the welcome night and the stars,
Over my cities shining all, enveloping man and land.


13

Sing on, sing on you gray-brown bird,
Sing from the swamps, the recesses, pour your chant from
     the bushes,
Limitless out of the dusk, out of the cedars and pines.

Sing on dearest brother, warble your reedy song,
Loud human song, with voice of uttermost woe.


O liquid and free and tender!
O wild and loose to my soul—O wondrous singer!
You only I hear—yet the star holds me, (but will **soon**
  depart,)
Yet the lilac with mastering odor holds me.


## 14

Now while I sat in the day and look'd forth,
In the close of the day with its light and the fields of spring,
  and the farmers preparing their crops,
In the large unconscious scenery of my land with its lakes
  and forests,
In the heavenly aerial beauty, (after the perturb'd winds
  and the storms,)
Under the arching heavens of the afternoon swift passing,
  and the voices of children and women,
The many-moving sea-tides, and I saw the ships how they
  sail'd,
And the summer approaching with richness, and the fields
  all busy with labor,
And the infinite separate houses, how they all went on, each
  with its meals and minutia of daily usages,
And the streets how their throbbings throbb'd, and the
  cities pent—lo, then and there,

Falling upon them all and among them all, enveloping me
    with the rest,
Appear'd the cloud, appear'd the long black trail,
And I knew death, its thought, and the sacred knowledge
    of death.


Then with the knowledge of death as walking one side of
    me,
And the thought of death close-walking the other side of
    me,
And I in the middle as with companions, and as holding the
    hands of companions,
I fled forth to the hiding receiving night that talks not,
Down to the shores of the water, the path by the swamp
    in the dimness,
To the solemn shadowy cedars and ghostly pines so still.


And the singer so shy to the rest receiv'd me,
The gray-brown bird I know receiv'd us comrades three,
And he sang the carol of death, and a verse for him I love.


From deep secluded recesses,
From the fragrant cedars and the ghostly pines so still,
Came the carol of the bird.


And the charm of the carol rapt me,
As I held as if by their hands my comrades in the night,
And the voice of my spirit tallied the song of the bird.

Come lovely and soothing death,
Undulate round the world, serenely arriving, arriving,
In the day, in the night, to all, to each,
Sooner or later delicate death.

Prais'd be the fathomless universe,
For life and joy, and for objects and knowledge curious,
And for love, sweet love—but praise! praise! praise!
For the sure-enwinding arms of cool-enfolding death.

Dark mother always gliding near with soft feet,
Have none chanted for thee a chant of fullest welcome?
Then I chant it for thee, I glorify thee above all,
I bring thee a song that when thou must indeed come, come
          unfalteringly.

Approach strong deliveress,
When it is so, when thou hast taken them I joyously sing
          the dead,
Lost in the loving floating ocean of thee,
Laved in the flood of thy bliss O death.

From me to thee glad serenades,
Dances for thee I propose saluting thee, adornments and
          feastings for thee,
And the sights of the open landscape and the high-spread
          sky are fitting,
And life and the fields, and the huge and thoughtful night.

298

The night in silence under many a star,
The ocean shore and the husky whispering wave whose
        voice I know,
And the soul turning to thee O vast and well-veil'd death,
And the body gratefully nestling close to thee.


Over the tree-tops I float thee a song,
Over the rising and sinking waves, over the myriad fields
        and the prairies wide,
Over the dense-pack'd cities all and the teeming wharves
        and ways,
I float this carol with joy, with joy to thee O death.


## 15

To the tally of my soul,
Loud and strong kept up the gray-brown bird,
With pure deliberate notes spreading filling the night.


Loud in the pines and cedars dim,
Clear in the freshness moist and the swamp-perfume,
And I with my comrades there in the night.


While my sight that was bound in my eyes unclosed,
As to long panoramas of visions.


And I saw askant the armies,
I saw as in noiseless dreams hundreds of battle-flags,

Borne through the smoke of the battles and pierc'd with
       missiles I saw them,
And carried hither and yon through the smoke, and torn
       and bloody,
And at last but a few shreds left on the staffs, (and all in
       silence,)
And the staffs all splinter'd and broken.

I saw battle-corpses, myriads of them,
And the white skeletons of young men, I saw them,
I saw the debris and debris of all the slain soldiers of the
       war,
But I saw they were not as was thought,
They themselves were fully at rest, they suffer'd not,
The living remain'd and suffer'd, the mother suffer'd,
And the wife and the child and the musing comrade suffer'd,
And the armies that remain'd suffer'd.

16

Passing the visions, passing the night,
Passing, unloosing the hold of my comrades' hands,
Passing the song of the hermit bird and the tallying song
       of my soul,
Victorious song, death's outlet song, yet varying ever-
       altering song,
As low and wailing, yet clear the notes, rising and falling,
       flooding the night,

Sadly sinking and fainting, as warning and warning, and
        yet again bursting with joy,
Covering the earth and filling the spread of the heaven,
As that powerful psalm in the night I heard from recesses,
Passing, I leave thee lilac with heart-shaped leaves,
I leave thee there in the door-yard, blooming, returning
        with spring.


I cease from my song for thee,
From my gaze on thee in the west, fronting the west, com-
        muning with thee,
O comrade lustrous with silver face in the night.


Yet each to keep and all, retrievements out of the night,
The song, the wondrous chant of the gray-brown bird,
And the tallying chant, the echo arous'd in my soul,
With the lustrous and drooping star with the countenance
        full of woe,
With the holders holding my hand nearing the call of the
        bird,
Comrades mine and I in the midst, and their memory ever
        to keep, for the dead I loved so well,
For the sweetest, wisest soul of all my days and lands—
        and this for his dear sake,
Lilac and star and bird twined with the chant of my soul,
There in the fragrant pines and the cedars dusk and dim.

# O CAPTAIN! MY CAPTAIN!

O Captain! my Captain! our fearful trip is done,
The ship has weather'd every rack, the prize we sought is
      won,
The port is near, the bells I hear, the people all exulting,
While follow eyes the steady keel, the vessel grim and
      daring;
            But O heart! heart! heart!
              O the bleeding drops of red,
                  Where on the deck my Captain lies,
                    Fallen cold and dead.


O Captain! my Captain! rise up and hear the bells;
Rise up—for you the flag is flung—for you the bugle trills,
For you bouquets and ribbon'd wreaths—for you the shores
      a-crowding,
For you they call, the swaying mass, their eager faces turn-
      ing;
            Here Captain! dear father!
              This arm beneath your head!
                  It is some dream that on the deck,
                    You've fallen cold and dead.


My Captain does not answer, his lips are pale and still,
My father does not feel my arm, he has no pulse nor will,
The ship is anchor'd safe and sound, its voyage closed and
      done,

From fearful trip the victor ship comes in with object won;
  Exult O shores, and ring O bells!
   But I with mournful tread,
    Walk the deck my Captain lies,
     Fallen cold and dead.


## HUSH'D BE THE CAMPS TO-DAY

*(May* 4, 1865.)

Hush'd be the camps to-day,
And soldiers let us drape our war-worn weapons,
And each with musing soul retire to celebrate,
Our dear commander's death.

No more for him life's stormy conflicts,
Nor victory, nor defeat—no more time's dark events,
Charging like ceaseless clouds across the sky.

But sing poet in our name,
Sing of the love we bore him—because you, dweller in
   camps, know it truly.

As they invault the coffin there,
Sing—as they close the doors of earth upon him—one verse,
For the heavy hearts of soldiers.

# THIS DUST WAS ONCE THE MAN

This dust was once the man,
Gentle, plain, just and resolute, under whose cautious hand,
Against the foulest crime in history known in any land or
      age,
Was saved the Union of these States.

# There Was A Child Went Forth

There was a child went forth every day,
And the first object he look'd upon, that object he became,
And that object became part of him for the day or a certain
   part of the day,
Or for many years or stretching cycles of years.

The early lilacs became part of this child,
And grass and white and red morning-glories, and white
   and red clover, and the song of the phœbe-bird,
And the Third-month lambs and the sow's pink-faint litter,
   and the mare's foal and the cow's calf,
And the noisy brood of the barnyard or by the mire of
   the pondside,
And the fish suspending themselves so curiously below
   there, and the beautiful curious liquid,
And the water-plants with their graceful flat heads, all
   became part of him.

The field-sprouts of Fourth-month and Fifth-month be-
   came part of him,
Winter-grain sprouts and those of the light-yellow corn, and
   the esculent roots of the garden,

And the apple-trees cover'd with blossoms and the fruit
       afterward, and wood-berries, and the commonest
       weeds by the road,
And the old drunkard staggering home from the outhouse
       of the tavern whence he had lately risen,
And the schoolmistress that pass'd on her way to the school,
And the friendly boys that pass'd, and the quarrelsome boys,
And the tidy and fresh-cheek'd girls, and the barefoot negro
       boy and girl,
And all the changes of city and country wherever he went.

His own parents, he that had father'd him and she that had
       conceiv'd him in her womb and birth'd him,
They gave this child more of themselves than that,
They gave him afterward every day, they became part of
       him.

The mother at home quietly placing the dishes on the
       supper-table,
The mother with mild words, clean her cap and gown, a
       wholesome odor falling off her person and clothes
       as she walks by,
The father, strong, self-sufficient, manly, mean, anger'd,
       unjust,
The blow, the quick loud word, the tight bargain, the crafty
       lure,
The family usages, the language, the company, the furni-
       ture, the yearning and swelling heart,
Affection that will not be gainsay'd, the sense of what is
       real, the thought if after all it should prove unreal,

The doubts of day-time and the doubts of night-time, the
    curious whether and how,
Whether that which appears so is so, or is it all flashes and
    specks?
Men and women crowding fast in the streets, if they are
    not flashes and specks what are they?
The streets themselves and the façades of houses, and goods
    in the windows,
Vehicles, teams, the heavy-plank'd wharves, the huge cross-
    ing at the ferries,
The village on the highland seen from afar at sunset, the
    river between,
Shadows, aureola and mist, the light falling on roofs and
    gables of white or brown two miles off,
The schooner near by sleepily dropping down the tide, the
    little boat slack-tow'd astern,
The hurrying tumbling waves, quick-broken crests, slap-
    ping,
The strata of color'd clouds, the long bar of maroon-tint
    away solitary by itself, the spread of purity it lies
    motionless in,
The horizon's edge, the flying sea-crow, the fragrance of
    salt marsh and shore mud,
These became part of that child who went forth every day,
    and who now goes, and will always go forth every
    day.

# To A Foil'd European Revolutionaire

Courage yet, my brother or my sister!
Keep on—Liberty is to be subserv'd whatever occurs;
That is nothing that is quell'd by one or two failures, or any
        number of failures,
Or by the indifference or ingratitude of the people, or by
        any unfaithfulness,
Or the show of the tushes of power, soldiers, cannon, penal
        statutes.

What we believe in waits latent forever through all the
        continents,
Invites no one, promises nothing, sits in calmness and light,
        is positive and composed, knows no discourage-
        ment,
Waiting patiently, waiting its time.

(Not songs of loyalty alone are these,
But songs of insurrection also,
For I am the sworn poet of every dauntless rebel the world
        over,
And he going with me leaves peace and routine behind him,
And stakes his life to be lost at any moment.)

The battle rages with many a loud alarm and frequent advance and retreat,
The infidel triumphs, or supposes he triumphs,
The prison, scaffold, garroté, handcuffs, iron necklace and leadballs do their work,
The named and unnamed heroes pass to other spheres,
The great speakers and writers are exiled, they lie sick in distant lands,
The cause is asleep, the strongest throats are choked with their own blood,
The young men droop their eyelashes toward the ground when they meet;
But for all this Liberty has not gone out of the place, nor the infidel enter'd into full possession.

When liberty goes out of a place it is not the first to go, nor the second or third to go,
It waits for all the rest to go, it is the last.

When there are no more memories of heroes and martyrs,
And when all life and all the souls of men and women are discharged from any part of the earth,
Then only shall liberty or the idea of liberty be discharged from that part of the earth,
And the infidel come into full possession.

Then courage European revolter, revoltress!
For till all ceases neither must you cease.

I do not know what you are for, (I do not know what I am
for myself, nor what any thing is for,)
But I will search carefully for it even in being foil'd,
In defeat, poverty, misconception, imprisonment—for they
too are great.

Did we think victory great?
So it is—but now it seems to me, when it cannot be help'd,
that defeat is great,
And that death and dismay are great.

# Proud Music of the Storm

## 1

Proud music of the storm,
Blast that careers so free, whistling across the prairies,
Strong hum of forest tree-tops—wind of the mountains,
Personified dim shapes—you hidden orchestras,
You serenades of phantoms with instruments alert,
Blending with Nature's rhythmus all the tongues of nations;
You chords left as by vast composers—you choruses,
You formless, free, religious dances—you from the Orient,
You undertone of rivers, roar of pouring cataracts,
You sounds from distant guns with galloping cavalry,
Echoes of camps with all the different bugle-calls,
Trooping tumultuous, filling the midnight late, bending me
       powerless,
Entering my lonesome slumber-chamber, why have you
       seiz'd me?

## 2

Come forward O my soul, and let the rest retire,
Listen, lose not, it is toward thee they tend,

Parting the midnight, entering my slumber-chamber,
For thee they sing and dance O soul.


A festival song,
The duet of the bridegroom and the bride, a marriage-
    march,
With lips of love, and hearts of lovers fill'd to the brim with
    love,
The red-flush'd cheeks and perfumes, the cortege swarming
    full of friendly faces young and old,
To flutes' clear notes and sounding harps' cantabile.


Now loud approaching drums,
Victoria! see'st thou in powder-smoke the banners torn but
    flying? the rout of the baffled?
Hearest those shouts of a conquering army?


(Ah soul, the sobs of women, the wounded groaning in
    agony,
The hiss and crackle of flames, the blacken'd ruins, the
    embers of cities,
The dirge and desolation of mankind.)


Now airs antique and mediæval fill me,
I see and hear old harpers with their harps at Welsh
    festivals,
I hear the minnesingers singing their lays of love,
I hear the minstrels, gleemen, troubadours, of the middle
    ages.

Now the great organ sounds,
Tremulous, while underneath, (as the hid footholds of the
      earth,
On which arising rest, and leaping forth depend,
All shapes of beauty, grace and strength, all hues we know,
Green blades of grass and warbling birds, children that
      gambol and play, the clouds of heaven above,)
The strong base stands, and its pulsations intermits not,
Bathing, supporting, merging all the rest, maternity of all
      the rest,
And with it every instrument in multitudes,
The players playing, all the world's musicians,
The solemn hymns and masses rousing adoration,
All passionate heart-chants, sorrowful appeals,
The measureless sweet vocalists of ages,
And for their solvent setting earth's own diapason,
Of winds and woods and mighty ocean waves,
A new composite orchestra, binder of years and climes, ten-
      fold renewer,
As of the far-back days the poets tell, the Paradiso,
The straying thence, the separation long, but now the
      wandering done,
The journey done, the journeyman come home,
And man and art with Nature fused again.


Tutti! for earth and heaven;
(The Almighty leader now for once has signal'd with his
      wand.)

The manly strophe of the husbands of the world,
And all the wives responding.

The tongues of violins,
(I think O tongues ye tell this heart, that cannot tell itself,
This brooding yearning heart, that cannot tell itself.)


3

Ah from a little child,
Thou knowest soul how to me all sounds became music,
My mother's voice in lullaby or hymn,
(The voice, O tender voices, memory's loving voices,
Last miracle of all, O dearest mother's, sister's, voices;)
The rain, the growing corn, the breeze among the long-
      leav'd corn,
The measur'd sea-surf beating on the sand,
The twittering bird, the hawk's sharp scream,
The wild-fowl's notes at night as flying low migrating north
      or south,
The psalm in the country church or mid the clustering trees,
      the open air camp-meeting,
The fiddler in the tavern, the glee, the long-strung sailor-
      song,
The lowing cattle, bleating sheep, the crowing cock at
      dawn.

All songs of current lands come sounding round me,
The German airs of friendship, wine and love,

Irish ballads, merry jigs and dances, English warbles,
Chansons of France, Scotch tunes, and o'er the rest,
Italia's peerless compositions.

Across the stage with pallor on her face, yet lurid passion,
Stalks Norma brandishing the dagger in her hand.

I see poor crazed Lucia's eyes' unnatural gleam,
Her hair down her back falls loose and dishevel'd.

I see where Ernani walking the bridal garden,
Amid the scent of night-roses, radiant, holding his bride by
        the hand,
Hears the infernal call, the death-pledge of the horn.

To crossing swords and gray hairs bared to heaven,
The clear electric base and baritone of the world,
The trombone duo, Libertad forever!

From Spanish chestnut trees' dense shade,
By old and heavy convent walls a wailing song,
Song of lost love, the torch of youth and life quench'd in
        despair,
Song of the dying swan, Fernando's heart is breaking.

Awaking from her woes at last retriev'd Amina sings,
Copious as stars and glad as morning light the torrents of
        her joy.

(The teeming lady comes,
The lustrious orb, Venus contralto, the blooming mother,
Sister of loftiest gods, Alboni's self I hear.)


4

I hear those odes, symphonies, operas,
I hear in the *William Tell* the music of an arous'd and angry
      people,
I hear Meyerbeer's *Huguenots,* the *Prophet,* or *Robert,*
Gounod's *Faust,* or Mozart's *Don Juan.*


I hear the dance-music of all nations,
The waltz, some delicious measure, lapsing, bathing me
      in bliss,
The bolero to tinkling guitars and clattering castanets.


I see religious dances old and new,
I hear the sound of the Hebrew lyre,
I see the crusaders marching bearing the cross on high, to
      the martial clang of cymbals,
I hear dervishes monotonously chanting, interspers'd with
      frantic shouts, as they spin around turning always
      towards Mecca,
I see the rapt religious dances of the Persians and the Arabs,
Again, at Eleusis, home of Ceres, I see the modern Greeks,
      dancing,
I hear them clapping their hands as they bend their bodies,
I hear the metrical shuffling of their feet.

I see again the wild old Corybantian dance, the performers
       wounding each other,
I see the Roman youth to the shrill sound of flageolets
       throwing and catching their weapons,
As they fall on their knees and rise again.

I hear from the Mussulman mosque the muezzin calling,
I see the worshippers within, nor form nor sermon, argu-
       ment nor word,
But silent, strange, devout, rais'd, glowing heads, ecstatic
       faces.

I hear the Egyptian harp of many strings,
The primitive chants of the Nile boatmen,
The sacred imperial hymns of China,
To the delicate sounds of the king, (the stricken wood and
       stone,)
Or to Hindu flutes and the fretting twang of the vina,
A band of bayaderes.

## 5

Now Asia, Africa leave me, Europe seizing inflates me,
To organs huge and bands I hear as from vast concourses of
       voices,
Luther's strong hymn *Eine feste Burg ist unser Gott,*
Rossini's *Stabat Mater dolorosa,*
Or floating in some high cathedral dim with gorgeous
       color'd windows,
The passionate *Agnus Dei* or *Gloria in Excelsis.*

Composers! mighty maestros!
And you, sweet singers of old lands, soprani, tenori, bassi!
To you a new bard caroling in the West,
Obeisant sends his love.

(Such led to thee O soul,
All senses, shows and objects, lead to thee,
But now it seems to me sound leads o'er all the rest.)

I hear the annual singing of the children in St. Paul's
       cathedral,
Or, under the high roof of some colossal hall, the sym-
       phonies, oratorios of Beethoven, Handel, or Haydn,
The *Creation* in billows of godhood laves me.

Give me to hold all sounds, (I madly struggling cry,)
Fill me with all the voices of the universe,
Endow me with their throbbings, Nature's also,
The tempests, waters, winds, operas and chants, marches
       and dances,
Utter, pour in, for I would take them all!

6

Then I woke softly,
And pausing, questioning awhile the music of my dream,
And questioning all those reminiscences, the tempest in its
       fury,

And all the songs of sopranos and tenors,
And those rapt oriental dances of religious fervor,
And the sweet varied instruments, and the diapason of
organs,
And all the artless plaints of love and grief and death,
I said to my silent curious soul out of the bed of the slumber-
chamber,
Come, for I have found the clew I sought so long,
Let us go forth refresh'd amid the day,
Cheerfully tallying life, walking the world, the real,
Nourish'd henceforth by our celestial dream.


And I said, moreover,
Haply what thou hast heard O soul was not the sound of
winds,
Nor dream of raging storm, nor sea-hawk's flapping wings
nor harsh scream,
Nor vocalism of sun-bright Italy,
Nor German organ majestic, nor vast concourse of voices,
nor layers of harmonies,
Nor strophes of husbands and wives, nor sound of march-
ing soldiers,
Nor flutes, nor harps, nor the bugle-calls of camps,
But to a new rhythmus fitted for thee,
Poems bridging the way from Life to Death, vaguely wafted
in night air, uncaught, unwritten,
Which let us go forth in the bold day and write.

# Passage to India

Singing my days,
Singing the great achievements of the present,
Singing the strong light works of engineers,
Our modern wonders, (the antique ponderous Seven
     outvied,)
In the Old World the east the Suez canal,
The New by its mighty railroad spann'd,
The seas inlaid with eloquent gentle wires;
Yet first to sound, and ever sound, the cry with thee O soul,
The Past! the Past! the Past!


The Past—the dark unfathom'd retrospect!
The teeming gulf—the sleepers and the shadows!
The past—the infinite greatness of the past!
For what is the present after all but a growth out of the
     past?
(As a projectile form'd, impell'd, passing a certain line,
     still keeps on,
So the present, utterly form'd, impell'd by the past.)

Passage O soul to India!
Eclaircise the myths Asiatic, the primitive fables.


Not you alone proud truths of the world,
Nor you alone ye facts of modern science,
But myths and fables of eld, Asia's, Africa's fables,
The far-darting beams of the spirit, the unloos'd dreams,
The deep diving bibles and legends,
The daring plots of the poets, the elder religions;
O you temples fairer than lilies pour'd over by the rising
       sun!
O you fables spurning the known, eluding the hold of the
       known, mounting to heaven!
You lofty and dazzling towers, pinnacled, red as roses,
       burnish'd with gold!
Towers of fables immortal fashion'd from mortal dreams!
You too I welcome and fully the same as the rest!
You too with joy I sing.


Passage to India!
Lo, soul, seest thou not God's purpose from the first?
The earth to be spann'd, connected by network,
The races, neighbors, to marry and be given in marriage,
The oceans to be cross'd, the distant brought near,
The lands to be welded together.


A worship new I sing,
You captains, voyagers, explorers, yours,

You engineers, you architects, machinists, yours,
You, not for trade or transportation only,
But in God's name, and for thy sake O soul.


3

Passage to India!
Lo soul for thee of tableaus twain,
I see in one the Suez canal initiated, open'd,
I see the procession of steamships, the Empress Eugenie's
        leading the van,
I mark from on deck the strange landscape, the pure sky, the
        level sand in the distance,
I pass swiftly the picturesque groups, the workmen gather'd,
The gigantic dredging machines.


In one again, different, (yet thine, all thine, O soul, the
        same,)
I see over my own continent the Pacific railroad surmounting
        every barrier,
I see continual trains of cars winding along the Platte
        carrying freight and passengers,
I hear the locomotives rushing and roaring, and the shrill
        steam-whistle,
I hear the echoes reverberate through the grandest scenery
        in the world,
I cross the Laramie plains, I note the rocks in grotesque
        shapes, the buttes,

I see the plentiful larkspur and wild onions, the barren, colorless, sage-deserts,

I see in glimpses afar or towering immediately above me the great mountains, I see the Wind river and the Wahsatch mountains,

I see the Monument mountain and the Eagle's Nest, I pass the Promontory, I ascend the Nevadas,

I scan the noble Elk mountain and wind around its base,

I see the Humboldt range, I thread the valley and cross the river,

I see the clear waters of lake Tahoe, I see forests of majestic pines,

Or crossing the great desert, the alkaline plains, I behold enchanting mirages of waters and meadows,

Marking through these and after all, in duplicate slender lines,

Bridging the three or four thousand miles of land travel,

Tying the Eastern to the Western sea,

The road between Europe and Asia.

( Ah Genoese thy dream! thy dream!

Centuries after thou are laid in thy grave,

The shore thou foundest verifies thy dream.)


4


Passage to India!

Struggles of many a captain, tales of many a sailor dead,

Over my mood stealing and spreading they come,

Like clouds and cloudlets in the unreach'd sky.

Along all history, down the slopes,
As a rivulet running, sinking now, and now again to the
      surface rising,
A ceaseless thought, a varied train—lo, soul, to thee, thy
      sight, they rise,
The plans, the voyages again, the expeditions;
Again Vasco de Gama sails forth,
Again the knowledge gain'd, the mariner's compass,
Lands found and nations born, thou born America,
For purpose vast, man's long probation fill'd,
Thou rondure of the world at last accomplish'd.


5

O vast Rondure, swimming in space,
Cover'd all over with visible power and beauty,
Alternate light and day and the teeming spiritual darkness,
Unspeakable high processions of sun and moon and count-
      less stars above,
Below, the manifold grass and waters, animals, mountains,
      trees,
With inscrutable purpose, some hidden prophetic intention,
Now first it seems my thought begins to span thee.


Down from the gardens of Asia descending radiating,
Adam and Eve appear, then their myriad progeny after
      them,
Wandering, yearning, curious, with restless explorations,

With questionings, baffled, formless, feverish, with never-
       happy hearts,
With that sad incessant refrain, *Wherefore unsatisfied soul?*
       and *Whither O mocking life?*


Ah who shall soothe these feverish children?
Who justify these restless explorations?
Who speak the secret of impassive earth?
Who bind it to us? what is this separate Nature so un-
       natural?
What is this earth to our affections? (unloving earth, with-
       out a throb to answer ours,
Cold earth, the place of graves.)


Yet soul be sure the first intent remains, and shall be carried
       out,
Perhaps even now the time has arrived.


After the seas are all cross'd (as they seem already cross'd,)
After the great captains and engineers have accomplish'd
       their work,
After the noble inventors, after the scientists, the chemist,
       the geologist, ethnologist,
Finally shall come the poet worthy that name,
The true son of God shall come singing his songs.


Then not your deeds only O voyagers, O scientists and
       inventors, shall be justified,
All these hearts as of fretted children shall be sooth'd,

All affection shall be fully responded to, the secret shall be
      told,
All these separations and gaps shall be taken up and hook'd
      and link'd together,
The whole earth, this cold, impassive, voiceless earth, shall
      be completely justified,
Trinitas divine shall be gloriously accomplish'd and com-
      pacted by the true son of God, the poet,
(He shall indeed pass the straits and conquer the mountains,
He shall double the cape of Good Hope to some purpose,)
Nature and Man shall be disjoin'd and diffused no more,
The true son of God shall absolutely fuse them.


6


Year at whose wide-flung door I sing!
Year of the purpose accomplish'd!
Year of the marriage of continents, climates and oceans!
(No mere doge of Venice now wedding the Adriatic,)
I see O year in you the vast terraqueous globe given and
      giving all,
Europe to Asia, Africa join'd, and they to the New World,
The lands, geographies, dancing before you, holding a
      festival garland,
As brides and bridegrooms hand in hand.


Passage to India!
Cooling airs from Caucasus far, soothing cradle of man,
The river Euphrates flowing, the past lit up again.

Lo soul, the retrospect brought forward,
The old, most populous, wealthiest of earth's lands,
The streams of the Indus and the Ganges and their many
      affluents,
(I my shores of America walking to-day behold, resuming
      all,)
The tale of Alexander on his warlike marches suddenly
      dying,
On one side China and on the other side Persia and Arabia,
To the south the great seas and the bay of Bengal,
The flowing literatures, tremendous epics, religions, castes,
Old occult Brahma interminably far back, the tender and
      junior Buddha,
Central and southern empires and all their belongings, pos-
      sessors,
The wars of Tamerlane, the reign of Aurungzebe,
The traders, rulers, explorers, Moslems, Venetians, Byzan-
      tium, the Arabs, Portuguese,
The first travelers famous yet, Marco Polo, Batouta the
      Moor,
Doubts to be solv'd, the map incognita, blanks to be fill'd,
The foot of man unstay'd, the hands never at rest,
Thyself O soul that will not brook a challenge.


The mediæval navigators rise before me,
The world of 1492, with its awaken'd enterprise,
Something swelling in humanity now like the sap of the
      earth in spring,
The sunset splendor of chivalry declining.

And who art thou sad shade?
Gigantic, visionary, thyself a visionary,
With majestic limbs and pious beaming eyes,
Spreading around with every look of thine a golden world,
Enhuing it with gorgeous hues.

As the chief histrion,
Down to the footlights walks in some great scena,
Dominating the rest I see the Admiral himself,
(History's type of courage, action, faith,)
Behold him sail from Palos leading his little fleet,
His voyage behold, his return, his great fame,
His misfortunes, calumniators, behold him a prisoner, chain'd,
Behold his dejection, poverty, death.

(Curious in time I stand, noting the efforts of heroes,
Is the deferment long? bitter the slander, poverty, death?
Lies the seed unreck'd for centuries in the ground? lo, to God's due occasion,
Uprising in the night, it sprouts, blooms,
And fills the earth with use and beauty.)


7

Passage indeed O soul to primal thought,
Not lands and seas alone, thy own clear freshness,
The young maturity of brood and bloom,
To realms of budding bibles.

O soul, repressless, I with thee and thou with me,
Thy circumnavigation of the world begin,
Of man, the voyage of his mind's return,
To reason's early paradise,
Back, back to wisdom's birth, to innocent intuitions,
Again with fair creation.


8

O we can wait no longer,
We too take ship O soul,
Joyous we too launch out on trackless seas,
Fearless for unknown shores on waves of ecstasy to sail,
Amid the wafting winds, (thou pressing me to thee, I thee
        to me, O soul,)
Caroling free, singing our song of God,
Chanting our chant of pleasant exploration.

With laugh and many a kiss,
(Let others deprecate, let others weep for sin, remorse,
        humiliation,)
O soul thou pleasest me, I thee.

Ah more than any priest O soul we too believe in God,
But with the mystery of God we dare not dally.

O soul thou pleasest me, I thee,
Sailing these seas or on the hills, or waking in the night,

Thoughts, silent thoughts, of Time and Space and Death,
    like waters flowing,
Bear me indeed as through the regions infinite,
Whose air I breathe, whose ripples hear, lave me all over,
Bathe me O God in thee, mounting to thee,
I and my soul to range in range of thee.


O Thou transcendent,
Nameless, the fibre and the breath,
Light of the light, shedding forth universes, thou centre of
    them,
Thou mightier centre of the true, the good, the loving,
Thou moral, spiritual fountain—affection's source—thou
    reservoir,
(O pensive soul of me—O thirst unsatisfied—waitest not
    there?
Waitest not haply for us somewhere there the Comrade per-
    fect?)
Thou pulse—thou motive of the stars, suns, systems,
That, circling, move in order, safe, harmonious,
Athwart the shapeless vastnesses of space,
How should I think, how breathe a single breath, how
    speak, if, out of myself,
I could not launch, to those, superior universes?


Swiftly I shrivel at the thought of God,
At Nature and its wonders, Time and Space and Death,
But that I, turning, call to thee O soul, thou actual Me,
And lo, thou gently masterest the orbs,

Thou matest Time, smilest content at Death,
And fillest, swellest full the vastnesses of Space.

Greater than stars or suns,
Bounding O soul thou journeyest forth;
What love than thine and ours could wider amplify?
What aspirations, wishes, outvie thine and ours O soul?
What dreams of the ideal? what plans of purity, perfection,
        strength?
What cheerful willingness for others' sake to give up all?
For others' sake to suffer all?

Reckoning ahead O soul, when thou, the time achiev'd,
The seas all cross'd, weather'd the capes, the voyage done,
Surrounded, copest, frontest God, yieldest, the aim attain'd,
As fill'd with friendship, love complete, the Elder Brother
        found,
The Younger melts in fondness in his arms.


9

Passage to more than India!
Are thy wings plumed indeed for such far flights?
O soul, voyagest thou indeed on voyages like those?
Disportest thou on waters such as those?
Soundest below the Sanscrit and the Vedas?
Then have thy bent unleash'd.

Passage to you, your shores, ye aged fierce enigmas!
Passage to you, to mastership of you, ye strangling problems!

331

You, strew'd with the wrecks of skeletons, that, living, never
      reach'd you.

Passage to more than India!
O secret of the earth and sky!
Of you O waters of the sea! O winding creeks and rivers!
Of you O woods and fields! of you strong mountains of my
      land!
Of you O prairies! of you gray rocks!
O morning red! O clouds! O rain and snows!
O day and night, passage to you!

O sun and moon and all you stars! Sirius and Jupiter!
Passage to you!

Passage, immediate passage! the blood burns in my veins!
Away O soul! hoist instantly the anchor!

Cut the hawsers—haul out—shake out every sail!
Have we not stood here like trees in the ground long
      enough?
Have we not grovel'd here long enough, eating and drink-
      ing like mere brutes?
Have we not darken'd and dazed ourselves with books long
      enough?

Sail forth—steer for the deep waters only,
Reckless O soul, exploring, I with thee, and thou with me,
For we are bound where mariner has not yet dared to go,
And we will risk the ship, ourselves and all.

O my brave soul!
O farther farther sail!
O daring joy, but safe! are they not all the seas of God?
O farther, farther, farther sail!

# Prayer of Columbus

A batter'd, wreck'd old man,
Thrown on this savage shore, far, far from home,
Pent by the sea and dark rebellious brows, twelve dreary
      months,
Sore, stiff with many toils, sicken'd and nigh to death,
I take my way along the island's edge,
Venting a heavy heart.


I am too full of woe!
Haply I may not live another day;
I cannot rest O God, I cannot eat or drink or sleep,
Till I put forth myself, my prayer, once more to Thee,
Breathe, bathe myself once more in Thee, commune with
      Thee,
Report myself once more to Thee.


Thou knowest my years entire, my life,
My long and crowded life of active work, not adoration
      merely;
Thou knowest the prayers and vigils of my youth,
Thou knowest my manhood's solemn and visionary medita-
      tions,

Thou knowest how before I commenced I devoted all to
   come to Thee,
Thou knowest I have in age ratified all those vows and
   strictly kept them,
Thou knowest I have not once lost nor faith nor ecstasy in
   Thee,
In shackles, prison'd, in disgrace, repining not,
Accepting all from Thee, as duly come from Thee.


All my emprises have been fill'd with Thee,
My speculations, plans, begun and carried on in thoughts
   of Thee,
Sailing the deep or journeying the land for Thee;
Intentions, purports, aspirations mine, leaving results to
   Thee.


O I am sure they really came from Thee,
The urge, the ardor, the unconquerable will,
The potent, felt, interior command, stronger than words,
A message from the Heavens whispering to me even in
   sleep,
These sped me on.


By me and these the work so far accomplish'd,
By me earth's elder cloy'd and stifled lands uncloy'd, un-
   loos'd,
By me the hemispheres rounded and tied, the unknown to
   the known.

The end I know not, it is all in Thee,
Or small or great I know not—haply what broad fields, what
    lands,
Haply the brutish measureless human undergrowth I know,
Transplanted there may rise to stature, knowledge worthy
    Thee,
Haply the swords I know may there indeed be turn'd to reap-
    ing-tools,
Haply the lifeless cross I know, Europe's dead cross, may
    bud and blossom there.


One effort more, my altar this bleak sand;
That Thou O God my life hast lighted,
With ray of light, steady, ineffable, vouchsafed of Thee,
Light rare untellable, lighting the very light,
Beyond all signs, descriptions, languages;
For that O God, be it my latest word, here on my knees,
Old, poor, and paralyzed, I thank Thee.


My terminus near,
The clouds already closing in upon me,
The voyage balk'd, the course disputed, lost,
I yield my ships to Thee.


My hands, my limbs grow nerveless,
My brain feels rack'd, bewilder'd,
Let the old timbers part, I will not part,
I will cling fast to Thee, O God, though the waves buffet me,
Thee, Thee at least I know.

Is it the prophet's thought I speak, or am I raving?
What do I know of life? what of myself?
I know not even my own work past or present,
Dim ever-shifting guesses of it spread before me,
Of newer better worlds, their mighty parturition,
Mocking, perplexing me.

And these things I see suddenly, what mean they?
As if some miracle, some hand divine unseal'd my eyes,
Shadowy vast shapes smile through the air and sky,
And on the distant waves sail countless ships,
And anthems in new tongues I hear saluting me.

# Darest Thou Now O Soul

Darest thou now O soul,
Walk out with me toward the unknown region,
Where neither ground is for the feet nor any path to follow?

No map there, nor guide,
Nor voice sounding, nor touch of human hand,
Nor face with blooming flesh, nor lips, nor eyes, are in that
     land.

I know it not O soul,
Nor dost thou, all is a blank before us,
All waits undream'd of in that region, that inaccessible land.

Till when the ties loosen,
All but the ties eternal, Time and Space,
Nor darkness, gravitation, sense, nor any bounds bounding
     us.

Then we burst forth, we float,
In Time and Space O soul, prepared for them,
Equal, equipt at last, (O joy! O fruit of all!) them to fulfil O
     soul.

# To One Shortly To Die

From all the rest I single out you, having a message for you,
You are to die—let others tell you what they please, I can-
      not prevaricate,
I am exact and merciless, but I love you—there is no escape
      for you.

Softly I lay my right hand upon you, you just feel it,
I do not argue, I bend my head close and half envelop it,
I sit quietly by, I remain faithful,
I am more than nurse, more than parent or neighbor,
I absolve you from all except yourself spiritual bodily, that
         is eternal, you yourself will surely escape,
The corpse you will leave will be but excrementitious.

The sun bursts through in unlooked-for directions,
Strong thoughts fill you and confidence, you smile,
You forget you are sick, as I forget you are sick,
You do not see the medicines, you do not mind the weeping
      friends, I am with you,
I exclude others from you, there is nothing to be commiser-
      ated,
I do not commiserate, I congratulate you.

339

# Thou Mother With Thy Equal Brood

Thou Mother with thy equal brood,
Thou varied chain of different States, yet one identity only,
A special song before I go I'd sing o'er all the rest,
For thee, the future.

I'd sow a seed for thee of endless Nationality,
I'd fashion thy ensemble including body and soul,
I'd show away ahead thy real Union, and how it may be ac-
        complish'd.

The paths to the house I seek to make,
But leave to those to come the house itself.

Belief I sing, and preparation;
As Life and Nature are not great with reference to the
        present only,
But greater still from what is yet to come,
Out of that formula for thee I sing.

As a strong bird on pinions free,
Joyous, the amplest spaces heavenward cleaving,
Such be the thought I'd think of thee America,
Such be the recitative I'd bring for thee.


The conceits of the poets of other lands I'd bring thee not,
Nor the compliments that have served their turn so long,
Nor rhyme, nor the classics, nor perfume of foreign court or
            indoor library;
But an odor I'd bring as from forests of pine in Maine, or
            breath of an Illinois prairie,
With open airs of Virginia or Georgia or Tennessee, or
            from Texas uplands, or Florida's glades,
Or the Saguenay's black stream, or the wide blue spread of
            Huron,
With presentment of Yellowstone's scenes, or Yosemite,
And murmuring under, pervading all, I'd bring the rustling
            sea-sound,
That endlessly sounds from the two Great Seas of the world.


And for thy subtler sense subtler refrains dread Mother,
Preludes of intellect tallying these and thee, mind-formulas
            fitted for thee, real and sane and large as these and
            thee,
Thou! mounting higher, diving deeper than we knew, thou
            transcendental Union!
By thee fact to be justified, blended with thought,

Thought of man justified, blended with God,
Through thy idea, lo, the immortal reality!
Through thy reality, lo, the immortal idea!


3

Brain of the New World, what a task is thine,
To formulate the Modern—out of the peerless grandeur of
      the modern,
Out of thyself, comprising science, to recast poems,
      churches, art,
(Recast, may-be discard them, end them—may-be their
      work is done, who knows?)
By vision, hand, conception, on the background of the
      mighty past, the dead,
To limn with absolute faith the mighty living present.


And yet thou living present brain, heir of the dead, the Old
      World brain,
Thou that lay folded like an unborn babe within its folds so
      long,
Thou carefully prepared by it so long—haply thou but un-
      foldest it, only maturest it,
It to eventuate in thee—the essence of the by-gone time con-
      tain'd in thee,
Its poems, churches, arts, unwitting to themselves, destined
      with reference to thee;
Thou but the apples, long, long, long a-growing,
The fruit of all the Old ripening to-day in thee.

## 4

Sail, sail thy best, ship of Democracy,
Of value is thy freight, 'tis not the Present only,
The Past is also stored in thee,
Thou holdest not the venture of thyself alone, not of the
        Western continent alone,
Earth's *résumé* entire floats on thy keel O ship, is steadied by
        thy spars,
With thee Time voyages in trust, the antecedent nations sink
        or swim with thee,
With all their ancient struggles, martyrs, heroes, epics, wars,
        thou bear'st the other continents,
Theirs, theirs as much as thine, the destination-port trium-
        phant;
Steer then with good strong hand and wary eye O helms-
        man, thou carriest great companions,
Venerable priestly Asia sails this day with thee,
And royal feudal Europe sails with thee.


5

Beautiful world of new superber birth that rises to my eyes,
Like a limitless golden cloud filling the western sky,
Emblem of general maternity lifted above all,
Sacred shape of the bearer of daughters and sons,
Out of thy teeming womb thy giant babes in ceaseless pro-
        cession issuing,

Acceding from such gestation, taking and giving continual
strength and life,
World of the real—world of the twain in one,
World of the soul, born by the world of the real alone, led
to identity, body, by it alone,
Yet in beginning only, incalculable masses of composite
precious materials,
By history's cycles forwarded, by every nation, language,
hither sent,
Ready, collected here, a freer, vast, electric world, to be
constructed here,
(The true New World, the world of orbic science, morals,
literatures to come,)
Thou wonder world yet undefined, unform'd, neither do I
define thee,
How can I pierce the impenetrable blank of the future?
I feel thy ominous greatness evil as well as good,
I watch thee advancing, absorbing the present, transcending
the past,
I see thy light lighting, and thy shadow shadowing, as if
the entire globe,
But I do not undertake to define thee, hardly to compre-
hend thee,
I but thee name, thee prophesy, as now,
I merely thee ejaculate!

Thee in thy future,
Thee in thy only permanent life, career, thy own unloosen'd
mind, thy soaring spirit,

Thee as another equally needed sun, radiant, ablaze, swift-
   moving, fructifying all,
Thee risen in potent cheerfulness and joy, in endless great
   hilarity,
Scattering for good the cloud that hung so long, that weigh'd
   so long upon the mind of man,
The doubt, suspicion, dread, of gradual, certain decadence
   of man;
Thee in thy larger, saner brood of female, male—thee in thy
   athletes, moral, spiritual, South, North, West, East,
(To thy immortal breasts, Mother of All, thy every daugh-
   ter, son, endear'd alike, forever equal,)
Thee in thy own musicians, singers, artists, unborn yet, but
   certain,
Thee in thy moral wealth and civilization, (until which thy
   proudest material civilization must remain in vain,)
Thee in thy all-supplying, all-enclosing worship—thee in no
   single bible, saviour, merely,
Thy saviours countless, latent within thyself, thy bibles in-
   cessant within thyself, equal to any, divine as any,
(Thy soaring course thee formulating, not in thy two great
   wars, nor in thy century's visible growth,
But far more in these leaves and chants, thy chants, great
   Mother!)
Thee in an education grown of thee, in teachers, studies,
   students, born of thee,
Thee in thy democratic fêtes en-masse, thy high original
   festivals, operas, lecturers, preachers,
Thee in thy ultimata, (the preparations only now completed,
   the edifice on sure foundations tied,)

Thee in thy pinnacles, intellect, thought, thy topmost
     rational joys, thy love and godlike aspiration,
In thy resplendent coming literati, thy full-lung'd orators,
     thy sacerdotal bards, kosmic savans,
These! these in thee, (certain to come,) to-day I prophesy.


6

Land tolerating all, accepting all, not for the good alone, all
     good for thee,
Land in the realms of God to be a realm unto thyself,
Under the rule of God to be a rule unto thyself.


(Lo, where arise three peerless stars,
To be thy natal stars my country, Ensemble, Evolution, Free-
     dom,
Set in the sky of Law.)


Land of unprecedented faith, God's faith,
Thy soil, thy very subsoil, all upheav'd,
The general inner earth so long so sedulously draped over,
     now hence for what it is boldly laid bare,
Open'd by thee to heaven's light for benefit or bale.


Not for success alone,
Not to fair-sail unintermitted always,
The storm shall dash thy face, the murk of war and worse
     than war shall cover thee all over,

(Wert capable of war, its tug and trials? be capable of peace, its trials,
For the tug and mortal strain of nations come at last in prosperous peace, not war;)
In many a smiling mask death shall approach beguiling thee, thou in disease shalt swelter,
The livid cancer spread its hideous claws, clinging upon thy breasts, seeking to strike thee deep within,
Consumption of the worst, moral consumption, shall rouge thy face with hectic,
But thou shalt face thy fortunes, thy diseases, and surmount them all,
Whatever they are to-day and whatever through time they may be,
They each and all shall lift and pass away and cease from thee,
While thou, Time's spirals rounding, out of thyself, thyself still extricating, fusing,
Equable, natural, mystical Union thou, (the mortal with immortal blent,)
Shalt soar toward the fulfilment of the future, the spirit of the body and the mind,
The soul, its destinies.

The soul, its destinies, the real real,
(Purport of all these apparitions of the real;)
In thee America, the soul, its destinies,
Thou globe of globes! thou wonder nebulous!
By many a throe of heat and cold convuls'd, (by these thyself solidifying,)

Thou mental, moral orb—thou New, indeed new, Spiritual
World!
The Present holds thee not—for such vast growth as thine,
For such unparallel'd flight as thine, such brood as thine,
The FUTURE only holds thee and can hold thee.

# To A Locomotive In Winter

Thee for my recitative,
Thee in the driving storm even as now, the snow, the winter-
       day declining,
Thee in thy panoply, thy measur'd dual throbbing and thy
       beat convulsive,
Thy black cylindric body, golden brass and silvery steel,
Thy ponderous side-bars, parallel and connecting rods,
       gyrating, shuttling at thy sides,
Thy metrical, now swelling pant and roar, now tapering in
       the distance,
Thy great protruding head-light fix'd in front,
Thy long, pale, floating vapor-pennants, tinged with deli-
       cate purple,
The dense and murky clouds out-belching from thy smoke-
       stack,
Thy knitted frame, thy springs and valves, the tremulous
       twinkle of thy wheels,
Thy train of cars behind, obedient, merrily following,
Through gale or calm, now swift, now slack, yet steadily
       careering;
Type of the modern—emblem of motion and power—pulse
       of the continent,

For once come serve the Muse and merge in verse, even as
        here I see thee,
With storm and buffeting gusts of wind and falling snow,
By day thy warning ringing bell to sound its notes,
By night thy silent signal lamps to swing.

Fierce-throated beauty!
Roll through my chant with all thy lawless music, thy swing-
        ing lamps at night,
Thy madly-whistled laughter, echoing, rumbling like an
        earthquake, rousing all,
Law of thyself complete, thine own track firmly holding,
(No sweetness debonair of tearful harp or glib piano thine,)
Thy trills of shrieks by rocks and hills return'd,
Launch'd o'er the prairies wide, across the lakes,
To the free skies unpent and glad and strong.

# So Long!

To conclude, I announce what comes after me.

I remember I said before my leaves sprang at all,
I would raise my voice jocund and strong with reference to
      consummations.

When America does what was promis'd,
When through these States walk a hundred millions of
      superb persons,
When the rest part away for superb persons and contribute
      to them,
When breeds of the most perfect mothers denote America,
Then to me and mine our due fruition.

I have press'd through in my own right,
I have sung the body and the soul, war and peace have I
      sung, and the songs of life and death,
And the songs of birth, and shown that there are many
      births.

I have offer'd my style to every one, I have journey'd with
      confident step;

While my pleasure is yet at the full I whisper *So long!*
And take the young woman's hand and the young man's
hand for the last time.


I announce natural persons to arise,
I announce justice triumphant,
I announce uncompromising liberty and equality,
I announce the justification of candor and the justification of
pride.


I announce that the identity of these States is a single identity
only,
I announce the Union more and more compact, indissoluble,
I announce splendors and majesties to make all the previous
politics of the earth insignificant.


I announce adhesiveness, I say it shall be limitless, un-
loosen'd,
I say you shall yet find the friend you were looking for.


I announce a man or woman coming, perhaps you are the
one, (*So long!*)
I announce the great individual, fluid as Nature, chaste,
affectionate, compassionate, fully arm'd.


I announce a life that shall be copious, vehement, spiritual,
bold,
I announce an end that shall lightly and joyfully meet its
translation.

I announce myriads of youths, beautiful, gigantic, sweet-
blooded,
I announce a race of splendid and savage old men.

O thicker and faster—(*So long!*)
O crowding too close upon me,
I foresee too much, it means more than I thought,
It appears to me I am dying.

Hasten throat and sound your last,
Salute me—salute the days once more. Peal the old cry once
more.

Screaming electric, the atmosphere using,
At random glancing, each as I notice absorbing,
Swiftly on, but a little while alighting,
Curious envelop'd messages delivering,
Sparkles hot, seed ethereal down in the dirt dropping,
Myself unknowing, my commission obeying, to question it
never daring,
To ages and ages yet the growth of the seed leaving,
To troops out of the war arising, they the tasks I have set
promulging,
To women certain whispers of myself bequeathing, their
affection me more clearly explaining,
To young men my problems offering—no dallier I—I the
muscle of their brains trying,
So I pass, a little time vocal, visible, contrary,
Afterward a melodious echo, passionately bent for, (death
making me really undying,)

The best of me then when no longer visible, for toward that
I have been incessantly preparing.

What is there more, that I lag and pause and crouch ex-
tended with unshut mouth?
Is there a single final farewell?

My songs cease, I abandon them,
From behind the screen where I hid I advance personally
solely to you.

Camerado, this is no book,
Who touches this touches a man,
(Is it night? are we here together alone?)
It is I you hold and who holds you,
I spring from the pages into your arms—decease calls me
forth.

O how your fingers drowse me,
Your breath falls around me like dew, your pulse lulls the
tympans of my ears,
I feel immerged from head to foot,
Delicious, enough.

Enough O deed impromptu and secret,
Enough O gliding present—enough O summ'd-up past.
Dear friend whoever you are take this kiss,
I give it especially to you, do not forget me,

I feel like one who has done work for the day to retire
   awhile,
I receive now again of my many translations, from my ava-
   taras ascending, while others doubtless await me,
An unknown sphere more real than I dream'd, more direct,
   darts awakening rays about me, *So long!*
Remember my words, I may again return,
I love you, I depart from materials,
I am as one disembodied, triumphant, dead.

# With Husky-Haughty Lips, O Sea!

With husky-haughty lips, O sea!
Where day and night I wend thy surf-beat shore,
Imaging to my sense thy varied strange suggestions,
(I see and plainly list thy talk and conference here,)
Thy troops of white-maned racers racing to the goal,
Thy ample, smiling face, dash'd with the sparkling dimples
      of the sun,
Thy brooding scowl and murk—thy unloos'd hurricanes,
Thy unsubduedness, caprices, wilfulness;
Great as thou art above the rest, thy many tears—a lack from
      all eternity in thy content,
(Naught but the greatest struggles, wrongs, defeats, could
      make thee greatest—no less could make thee,)
Thy lonely state—something thou ever seek'st and seek'st,
      yet never gain'st,
Surely some right withheld—some voice, in huge monoto-
      nous rage, of freedom-lower pent,
Some vast heart, like a planet's, chain'd and chafing in those
      breakers,
By lengthen'd swell, and spasm, and panting breath,
And rhythmic rasping of thy sands and waves,
And serpent hiss, and savage peals of laughter,

And undertones of distant lion roar,
(Sounding, appealing to the sky's deaf ear—but now, rap-
        port for once,
A phantom in the night thy confidant for once,)
The first and last confession of the globe,
Outsurging, muttering from thy soul's abysms,
The tale of cosmic elemental passion,
Thou tellest to a kindred soul.

56146